AF351518

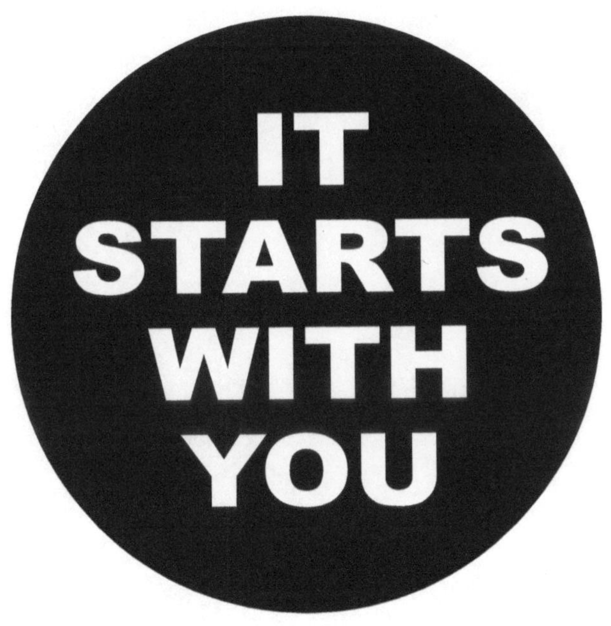

IT
STARTS
WITH
YOU

Authored by

BHARAT DAGA

Disclaimer

This book has been published with all reasonable efforts taken to make the material error-free after the consent of the author. This book is sold subject to the condition that it shall not, by way of trade or otherwise, be lent, resold, or otherwise circulated without the copyright owner's prior written consent in any form of binding or cover other than that in which it is published and without a similar condition including this condition being imposed on the subsequent purchaser and without limiting the rights under copyright reserved above, no part of this publication maybe reproduced, stored in or introduced into a retrieval system or transmitted in any form or by any other means without the permission of the copyright owner.

SUPER FAST AUTHOR

www.superfastauthor.com

Registered Office- 604, Mayur Vatika, Dapodi Pune 411001
Website: https://www.superfastauthor.com
Email: superfastauthor@gmail.com

First Published by SUPERFASTAUTHOR 2020

Copyright © BHARAT DAGA 2020

Title: IT STARTS WITH YOU
Price: INR 599 / $ 11.99
All Rights Reserved.
ISBN 978-93-90174-02-7

LIMITS OF LIABILITY/DISCLAIMER OF WARRANTY

Dedication

This book is dedicated to all my business owner
friends who are the super-heroes for this book
so that we all can find success more easily
and with much lesser efforts.

Acknowledgement

This book is a result of so many people who have been a part of my life directly and indirectly who helped me put together my thoughts to be able to make it into this book form.

To help me try and not forget anyone, I shall divide the acknowledgement section into professional and personal.

PROFESSIONAL ACKNOWLEDGEMENTS –

I would like to definitely start off with acknowledging BNI as an organisation which helped me find myself and giving me a chance and opportunity to grow as a person.

When I mention BNI, I cannot but say thank you to the founder of BNI, Dr. Ivan Misner who has given all of us the basic principles of networking and every time I had an opportunity to meet or hear him speak was an opportunity to learn more about so many subjects covered in this book.

Thank you to our CEO of BNI Graham Weihmiller, who opened my mind up to new ideas and a different style of leadership through his unique management styles in BNI.

My thanks are due to so many trainers, mentors, friends and guides in BNI who helped me learn so much more about networking like Mac Srinivasan, YP Lai, Phil Berg, Michael Mayer, Harald Lais, Tim Cook, Aqil Radjab, KVT Ramesh, Sunil Sethia through their personal conversations with me and their training and speeches.

One name that is missing in the list above is of Murali Sundaram who changed my entire way of thinking through his training and also teaching us selflessly about how to become one of the best trainers that we can.

I would also like to thank Mike Macedonio, Dawn Lyons and Eddie Espito from Asentiv who started me off on discovering my why and a lot of life stories were through a workshop conducted by them. I would also like to add my thanks to Bharat Jethani, who is the current head of Asentiv in Central India and also Abhijit Bam who was my trainer when I attended the course in India of Asentiv.

My thanks to Lois Weinblatt for a one-day workshop on visioning, which was the origin of my thoughts of having this journey of writing a book.

Thank you to Kailash Pinjani, my book coach who has been incredibly patient with me as I must be one of his only clients who did not follow the superfast author timeline, but he never gave up on me.

My professional acknowledgements would be incomplete without mentioning the 1000's of business owners who have had conversations with me and also listened to me patiently so that I could gather material for this book and see what worked and what did not to be able to share it you. Some of *them who encouraged me and one name in particular over here is Advocate Anand Mahurkar who only asked me one question every time I met him for one whole year and that was about me writing a book.*

PERSONAL ACKNOWLEDGEMENTS –

I will have to start this off my first and foremost thanking my grandfather Shri Ranglalji Daga who is no more here with us physically but has left his teachings behind with me with all the time spent with me and his lovely talks with me. I cherish the time spent with him and wish that I could have had some more time to learn from him.

Next is someone who is missing from above in the professional acknowledgements and that is because this is a personal acknowledgement to my partner and co-executive Director in BNI, Atul Joglekar who has always given me the support and the backing for me to explore my dreams and thoughts and is like the brick wall always behind me.

I would like to thank my parents next who are the ones responsible for what I am today too. My father Mr. Ashoke Daga is a cancer survivor and his life taught me a lesson that nothing and no one can ever keep you down if you refuse to stay down. My mother, Mrs. Urmila Daga, who as a homemaker showed me her undying and unquestioned love through my thick and thins of life and what selfless giving looks like.

Last but not least, a big thank you to my biggest supporter and my undying source of motivation and action, My Wife, Yamini Deshmukh. This book would probably not have seen the light of the day without the relentless persuasion by Yamini for me to take the time out and finish this. And whenever I was stuck or I had stopped, to not only read what I had written but to spend so many hours just making me re-think and starting off on this again.

One last thank you to my global group of "best friends" where each one of them have backed me at so many different times of my journey.

That is a lot of thank you's, but there are so many more missing who made this book possible by being a part of my life at various moments of time to remind me that "it all starts with me".

Thank you.

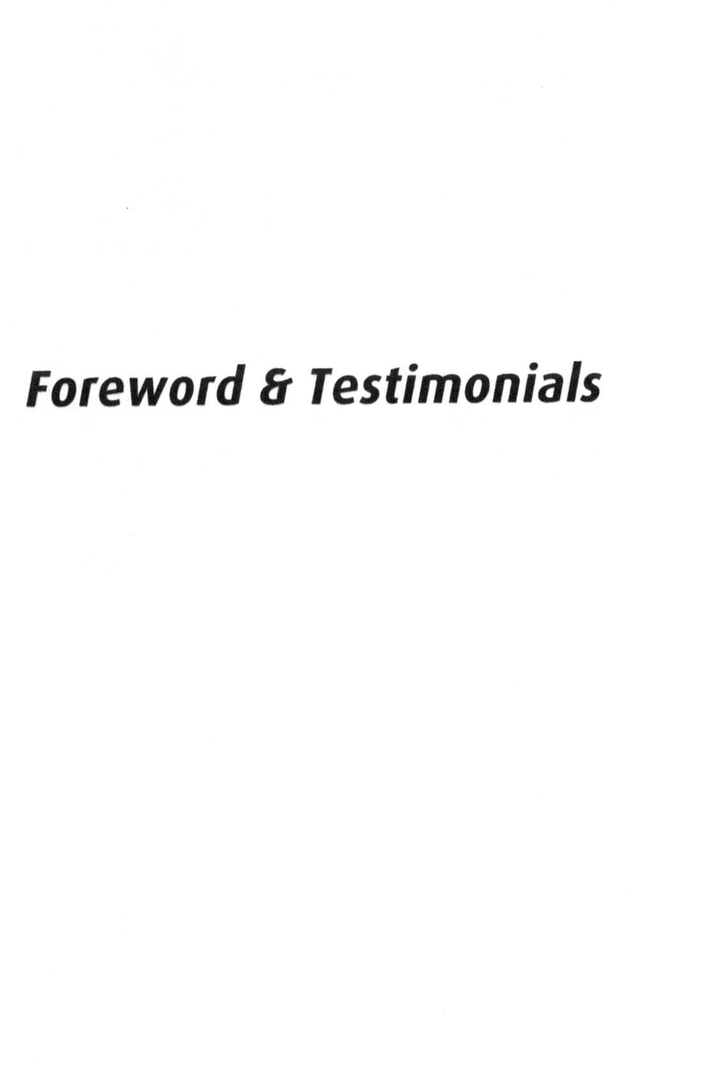
Foreword & Testimonials

From the Desk of Ivan Misner

"First, you have to be visible in the community.
You have to get out there and connect with people.
It's not called net-sitting or net-eating.
It's called networking. You have to work at it."

– Ivan Misner

I first met Bharat at the 2014 BNI Global Conference, which was his first global convention. I saw this humble looking, almost lost, person who came up to me after the awards ceremony to tell me that he simply loved BNI and everything about it. Then he said that next year his region would also be in the top 10 regions in the world as this would help his regional members to get more connects and grow their businesses. My first reaction was, "It's good to have goals." That is when he introduced himself as Bharat Daga, a new BNI Executive Director from India. He also went on to say that nothing would please him more than to be recognised on stage with me as he considered me his mentor relating to Givers Gain® and this would help him increase the level of giving to his members.

I get a lot of people coming up to me every year at the global convention and introducing themselves, but it is not common that someone commits to doing something at a convention and then they actually exceed that commitment. Bharat proved himself and I did get a chance to recognise him in the top 10 regions in the world the very next year.

Since then, I have seen him grow in BNI in many ways. He has been a global convention speaker every year since then. He has also trained BNI members and leaders internationally. He participates in many inclusive leadership model groups in BNI, the Founders Circle and the Innovation Task Force amongst them.

I have listened to his presentations at the Global Convention and I have found that his ideas, and his way of communicating them through stories, helps people understand his messages clearly and easily learn from him. This helps his audience get motivated, take action, and get better results.

It gives me great pleasure to say that he has brought this same style to his first book called "It Starts With You".

There are books which motivate you and there are books that help you work on yourself. This book is a perfect blend of personal stories for motivation, and also encourages you to think about and work on your own business. The book is like a roadmap for entrepreneurs to start thinking about themselves and to learn to effectively communicate, which will help them connect with others so that more people around them can become catalysts in their success. The book takes you through this whole journey with a step by step approach through simple exercises and examples. It is easy to understand and practical in its approach, and that is why it can produce the promised results.

I strongly recommend this book for any entrepreneur who wants to reap the benefits from networking; even though networking is not the main topic, the book covers all the steps you need before you start networking to make it even more fruitful for you. The time you spend exploring the ideas of communication and connecting that are in this book can produce massive results for you when you start using them in BNI and at any other networks that you might be a part of.

Ivan R. Misner, Ph.D.
Founder of BNI
New York Times Bestselling Author

From the Desk of Graham Weihmiller

*"Great Leaders do not tell you what to do.
They show you how it's done"*

– *Graham Weihmiller*

If you are reading these words, you are a person who is interested in self-improvement. You are seeking to have a greater impact on your family, your business, and your community. You also want to leave a positive legacy in the world. Sound familiar? Good. Because you are reading the right book from the right author.

I have had the distinct honor of working alongside Mr. Bharat Daga for years. He embodies and exemplifies the greatest qualities to which we as global business leaders can aspire. He is humble to a fault yet a well-traveled and well-respected global business executive. He is a terrific listener and open to new ideas and ways of thinking yet someone whom others actively seek out for advice. He is successful at whatever he puts his mind to yet he always put the interests of others before his own. In short, he is the person many of us would like to be. By internalizing what he teaches us, we have a chance to get one step closer to the people we want to be.

It is an important time for us to carefully review this work. The world needs thoughtful, proactive leaders more than ever before. I believe business leaders must lead the way forward – and they must do so exemplifying the philosophies embodied in this book. I am thankful to Bharat for so many things. Now I'm also thankful to him for sharing more of his wisdom in the following pages. My friends: let us now learn together and put into practice what he teaches us. Onward!

Graham Weihmiller
Chairman & CEO of BNI

From the Desk of Marshall Goldsmith

"To help others develop, start with yourself."

– Marshall Goldsmith

I had a chance to meet Bharat first at the BNI Indian Leadership Conference in 2018 in Mumbai, and subsequently again at my training event in the same tour.

In my conversations with him, I keenly remember that he was impacted by my work and by my keynote, where I had talked about creating millions of other mentors to help individuals reach their greatest heights. He also asked me how could he contribute in this mission I had to impact more lives and help more leaders (especially entrepreneurs) become successful. He believed that this was a difficult and lonely journey, and he wanted to help make connecting and communicating effectively easier for them.

I was excited that someone wanted to know more about how to impact the lives of these leaders and also saw that he was focused in his approach. He was clear of where he wanted to create change, so I told him to continue speaking to entrepreneurs and to write down his ideas, so that millions of others could learn from his thoughts.

I am delighted that he followed up by writing his first book, It Starts With You. This book is filled with useful, practical and insightful knowledge of how to take your career and leadership to the next level through more clear and effective networking.

This is a powerful book, though the concepts may seem simple. Bharat has simplified the ideas so that they are easy to understand and apply to your life. This is what I love best about this book. It doesn't have to be rocket science to learn to take yourself to the next level!

I would recommend this book to anyone that would like to start mapping out their future and taking control of it. This is also a key tool for improving networking and creating successful opportunities through your network.

I am keenly looking forward to what comes next from this simple, but powerful, author.

Marshall Goldsmith

Marshall Goldsmith is the New York Times #1 bestselling author of Triggers, Mojo, and What Got You Here Won't Get You There.

Marshall Goldsmith - Thinkers 50 #1 Executive Coach and only two-time #1 Leadership Thinker in the world.

"This book is a must read for not only entrepreneurs but also for young employees especially in the sales and marketing field. For Start-up entrepreneurs, the book could be like a roadmap for success. This book helps to make sure that not only do you understand yourself and why are you doing what you are doing but also but also how to use that to reach your goals. I would like to specially mention that what is different in this book is that it is a step by step approach for getting success and not just thoughts/ideas or stories."

Mr. M.S. Unnikrishnan
Managing Director & CEO, Thermax Ltd.

*****

Well compiled. Getting Successful is not a big challenge as much as sustaining the success in long run. Fast, bright and positive brains radiate more when interact with intellectuals with intense focus. This book recalls my early learning "Taste of water is purely from the soil it has been coming or running". Mr Bharat Daga has highlighted two essential aspects of happiness and prosperity 1. Be good enough for people come to you often. 2. Be wise enough to understand whom to be with. Either helps you to be in "highway". Both puts you in "runway"

Met high energy, focused, humorous Mr Daga in many BNI events and I am delighted to read his book that can add value in entrepreneurial journey. Focus on right people, Learn right values, Grow fast and better and Enjoy every minute of life.

Dr A Velumani PhD.,
Creator, Thyrocare. @velumania

*****

"Beware. This is NOT a BOOK. This is actually a Workbook for every Entrepreneur in the world. Most of the books on Entrepreneurship are motivational and inspire them to focus on the "WHY". But very few authors in the world actually guides the business owners on what and HOW to do. This BOOK is filled with loads of worksheets and templates and when applying all the principles and strategies, this BOOK can 100% HELP any business owner to understand who they truly are, what they really need to do, how to communicate in the right way to get things done and scale up their business. Bharat Daga is an amazing friend of mine for many years and I am so proud of this accomplishment in penning down his 30+ yrs of experience in a very simple and easy way to learn and apply. I have personally learnt a lot from his Entrepreneurial wisdom and I am sure each and one of you will get benefited from this book."

Murali Sundaram, Happiness Coach®,
Author & Global Master Trainer
(www.HappynessCoach.co.in)

*****

Preface

Every book should have a reason to be written!
The reason why I wanted to write my first book on this topic was because it has resonated with me all my life that there definitely has to be an easier way to become successful in life and the more I kept thinking about it, I was lucky to be pushed that way through life.

I was fortunate to have entered BNI when I was about 38 years of age and mildly successful. I had a world of experience and practical knowledge by having tried my hand at many things as an entrepreneur.

I have always been an avid reader and had spent considerable money even when I had limited means to get more information and even more as I could keep reading more and more and at one point of time, I was going through 1 book a week.

In spite of this, I was only mildly successful, and I wondered what was missing in the whole knowledge search. It took me 6 more years of learning networking in BNI that I realised what was missing started with me and with having a world of only outside knowledge but also knowledge about oneself, and that is why the title of the book is "It Starts With You."

To this got added some years of meeting many more people and networking and this was the next missing link which got connected, It was about me and connecting with people around me that could lead to an easier path to success. That was a great start, but how do you connect the two was something I still had to find out.

As Marshal Goldsmith says that it takes close 10000 hours of practice to really excel at something. I was lucky to have had a chance to become an Executive Director with BNI in the year 2013 and this gave me access to more business-owners and working with them and speaking to them and interviewing them and most importantly learn from them. The last 4 years have been the best learning years understanding the business challenges and opportunities of business owners across the world and working to finding solutions together. I also got the chance to work with some of the fantastic leaders across the organisation who made me think deeper as we explored pushing the limits of performance and our visions to even greater heights.

This book is my attempt of sharing with you the 10000 hours of work combined with all my personal learnings as a business owner, being a lifelong learner fortunate to have access and worked closely with many other business leaders; and a chance to guide and train entrepreneurs.

Hope you find your path of success and happiness more easily.

Index

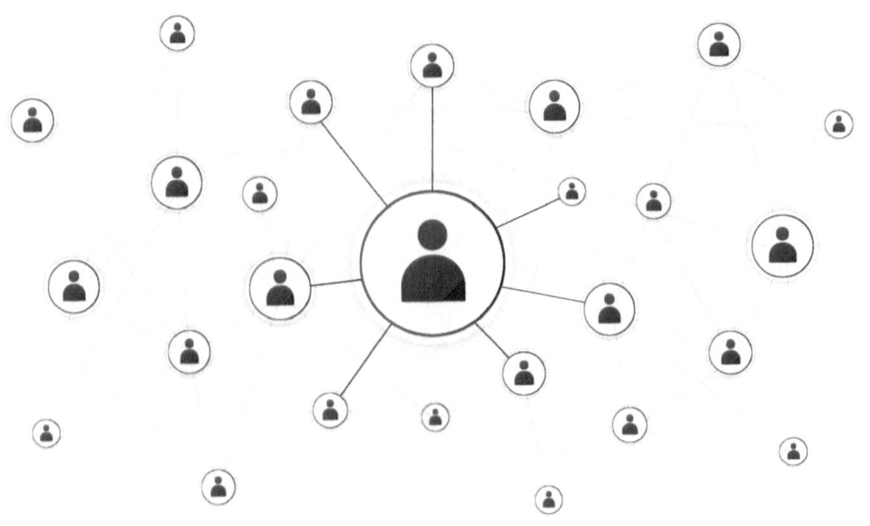

CHAPTER

One

Why are you in Business?

Let's start our journey of this book together with a flashback.

The year was 1990 and I had finished my graduation in commerce and joined my father's textile business which was in Ahmedabad. All throughout my college days, I had been visiting the office and learnt various aspects of the business and so it was logical to join it.

However, the business was not doing well due to our non-ability to compete with smaller firms and the overheads of doing business ethically and so we were losing money in a big way and were close to being bankrupt after my father had invested all his savings and funds that he had collected in almost 20 years of employment into the business.

The decision was finally taken one day when we realised that there wasn't any more money left to be invested in trying and turning it around and as my father was better qualified, he could get a job which would be better for the family.

He would leave the business and take up a job and I would try and handle the business.

This was one of the first learnings of my life. One of the easiest decisions was that I was able to accept defeat and failure and so I decided to cut my losses, learn and move ahead. I realised that I would not be able to turn my business around; thus, it might be a better idea to just shut the shop. My lesson learnt was to accept your losses and move ahead in your life as there are other things to do.

That is exactly what I did and was able to wind up the activities of our business. But we had a huge amount of creditors and also the bank dues which had to be cleared. For this, my father was sending the funds so the outstanding payments could be settled in parts, with me handling the transactions.

I still remember the time when as a 26-year-old, I had to handle this all alone and feel the chills down my spine today thinking of how I did it.

What I remember the most in this whole story was that acute *"feeling of loneliness"* when I had no one to speak about what I was going through. I did not want to tell my wife as I did not want to transfer the stress that I was facing to anyone else. Trust me that no one likes to tell their friend circle that they are a failure as you feel that you might just become the talk of the town for being a failure.

Across many years of speaking to many business owners, I found that at most stages of their entrepreneurship journey, nearly all business owners felt that they were lonely and always felt that they had to handle the matters all alone and were struggling to find someone to speak too.

You cannot take your problems home till you absolutely do not have too, as you do not want to give stress at home and there are so many other things that need attention at home like children, plans, parents and illnesses.

You cannot speak about your problems to your employees as they would just start looking at other options. And surely, we cannot even think of speaking about this to our bankers as they would want their funds back that very day itself.

The fact is that Entrepreneurship is a lonely journey!

So, why do entrepreneurs continue pursuing their dreams?

Having asked this to countless business owners, the biggest difference of why people stayed on in their business in spite of all the odds is only linked to one answer and that is that they knew their "*WHY*", all along.

Currently, I am part of an organisation called BNI which stands for Business Network International and I am in this business after going through 7 other businesses earlier. I have managed to stay with this business for almost 13 years and now enjoy every minute of it. In spite of all the odds, this was the answer to my story that Entrepreneurship does not have to be a lonely journey.

BNI builds business communities for collaborative growth. It helps business owners come together to work together as a team. This growth is not only business growth but also for personal development. BNI is based on the strong principle of bonding and relationships;

you get to build new relationships, new friends and new business associates.

Every day in BNI, I hear stories of how business owners have helped other business owners and supported them on their journey of being an entrepreneur. It could be through referrals for growth of the business or giving connections for collaboration to expand their business and even at times through simple ideas.

Every time I hear such stories, it feeds "my being" as I believe that together we can make the world of business owners less lonely and more fulfilling.

I have also found that most of the times, those business owners who are clear about why are they in the business get this help and support from others more easily and this was one of the reasons I got inspired to write this book.

Those who start finding their why get closer to people who help them get to their why and so let's start first with your why?

DO YOU KNOW YOUR WHY?

Having asked business owners why are they in business, the first answer you get is, to make money or profits.

But the deeper you go into it, you find that the excellent business owners and the ones making most of the money are the ones who have a deeper "WHY".

How do you find your Why?

The 6 Why Process -

Let's try and find your why by following the 6 Why process and see if we can connect your inner self to your business.

Ready for a small exercise?

Why are you doing your business, or why do you want to start a business? (write down your reason below)

Why is the above important for you?

Why is that so?

Why?

Why?

....

....

....

....

Why?

....

....

....

....

By now you must have distilled your "*why*" and some of you might have reached the reason why you are doing what you are doing today even before the 6 why's got over.

However, I would request you to try and reach the 6th level of why even if it feels uncomfortable and repetitive, as that will define why you are what you are doing today.

Each "*why*" gives you further clarity to get to your reason.

There could be some more things that you might need to add to clarify your why and now let's have a look at them:

WHAT EXCITES YOU ABOUT WHAT YOU ARE DOING?

Let me answer first to give you an idea:-

What excites me about the work I do through BNI with business owners is that I give them an opportunity amongst other things to make sure that they can form a team around the people who might be going through what they are going through and discuss it.

This could be possible if they are in the same industry or have the same kind of clients or what we technically call the same target market or they could be in the same stage of their business.

Now, it's your turn

Tell yourself what is exciting about what you do in the lines below.

....

....

....

....

WHAT DOES NOT EXCITE YOU ABOUT WHAT YOU ARE DOING?

An interesting way to answer this question could be:-

What don't you like about what you are doing currently?

This will tell you which parts of your business pull you down and will not help in bringing the excitement in doing what you are doing every day.

This answer can also help you find how to get rid of that part, and we shall cover this in the later portions of the book.

Now time to write this down.

What does not excite you about what you are doing?

....

....

....

....

WHY DO YOU DO WHAT YOU DO?

It should be obvious by now as you must have realised your "*why*" and some of you must have also realised your "***why not***".

I apologise if you found more reasons in the "***why not*** "compared to the "*why*".

This will just open a chasm in your life and you will be able to compare "why are you doing what you are doing" with "what you should be doing" that helps you find and achieve your "*why*".

In simple terms, all I am saying is that if you cannot find your "why" for whatever you are doing today in your life, you will keep doing it and switching it till you find your "***why***"?

I have always wanted to be in a sales job but kept wondering why I needed to keep finding something new?

I started my career with Textile manufacturing, but manufacturing was just not my cup of tea/coffee or even hot chocolate, changing to marketing floppy diskettes, moving on to the next stage of selling plastic granules and then back to selling textiles. And finally, I moved on to selling Financial Products.

Throughout my career, if I look back now, I feel that more than selling I was trying to find solutions, how can I help the person in front of me to be able to solve his problem, or even make more money by investing in the product or service I was offering to them. Quite often, this feeling of mine got in the way of being a sales-person though it helped me build wonderful relationships with people. I thought at times that maybe sales were not for me but gradually across time, I started feeling comfortable with sales.

Along came BNI in my life and when I joined as a member, I started getting a chance to connect with people. My approach to finding solutions to help people started paying off over here. It became an integral part of my life even before BNI became part of my business as I was drawn to listening to other business owners and their struggles and challenges and how they were overcoming them.

I met so many interesting people, for example:- a member that I knew whose father was a rickshaw driver. He started off as a mechanic, and today he owns a business of pumping solutions where he is planning to purchase his first Mercedes.

Stories like these inspire me to see the people who connect with their *"why"*, and because of this, they keep finding potential customers and thus they keep growing.

It was fascinating to see how one member speaks to another and they help each other grow and reach beyond themselves. I was finally able to share my learnt knowledge and put all the books that I had been reading, to use for others. It was like I was living life high on some drug.

Then came the opportunity to own the BNI business and that was when I needed to rethink whether it was something that "*I*" wanted to do and did I want to give myself up to this, completely knowing that facing fresh challenges and finding new opportunities was in my blood.

WHAT DO YOU DO IN YOUR BUSINESS THAT CONNECTS WITH YOUR INNER THOUGHTS AND FEELINGS?

Can you feel "*the story of*" how your business actually connects with you as a person?

Let me continue the story of BNI becoming my business from where I left it in the earlier section, which might help explain what I mean when I say that a business should connect with some inner thoughts of your life.

When this decision point of whether BNI should be taken up as a business came into my life, it was a sleepless night that helped me make my decision.

Let me share this one incident from my life which I remembered that night and helped me make my decision.

After we had closed down our business and settled everything related to that, I was left with nothing to do and that is when one of the biggest influencers of my life took me under his wing and that was my grandfather.

I started working with him as a part of handling his

business. He owned a business where he had a textile agency of Century Textile Mills and was the sole selling agent for regions in Maharashtra.

My grandfather was settled in Mumbai at that time and I was living in Ahmedabad. I used to visit him to learn from him and I also used to accompany him on the sales tour with the company representatives.

On one such trip to Mumbai, my grandfather and I left the house to go to the office. The residence was at Altamount Road (which is now considered as one of top 10 expensive streets of the world with the likes of Ambani residing in that area) and our office was at Nariman point (again one of the most posh office addresses in Mumbai where MNC & Foreign banks had their India offices).

We left home and started walking and I knew that, since my grandfather was old and could not drive, we might be finding a cab/taxi to go to the office. After walking for almost about a kilometre, we reached a bus stop and I was surprised that we were standing at a bus stop. In India, normally, the well off people do not travel by bus. I thought we were comfortable with money, considering where we lived? When the bus came, we got onto it and seeing a senior citizen; we got a place to sit.

I remember vividly as I turned around to my grandfather and asked him as to why we were travelling by bus considering the fact that I thought we could easily afford a better option.

The first response of my grandfather was to ask me if

I was uncomfortable, we could get off at the next stop and take a taxi. I told him that I was okay and just wanted to know why my grandfather travelled by a public bus.

My Grandfather replied that the simple answer was that currently, he could afford this and so he wanted to try this. That is when I asked him about his properties and he replied that the house belonged to my grandmother as he had gifted it to her completely and the office belonged to his other grandchildren and me as he had made living trust and so the property was not his.

This was said by the person who had helped our family in times of trouble by giving us funds and by helping us come out of the financial mess of our earlier business.

It was not the words alone which touched me but the smile and serenity of his face which I can still remember that made me realise the power and the feeling that a simple act of "Giving" could give to any of us.

This connected me with the core philosophy of BNI - Givers Gain®

My reason for "*WHY*" I connected with BNI became very clear to me that night and every time I feel tired or frustrated, I just have to think back to the time where my grandfather taught me the first reason for doing anything in life.

And that is certainly a very different thought that helps me decide about anything I think about doing now !!

I would like to thank and am grateful to many people for helping me find "*my why*" and foremost amongst them are Ivan Misner, Mike Macedonia, Dawn Lyons and Eddie Espito who are the founders of Asentiv where they helped me discover the truths about myself through their courses and with help from my friend Bharat Jethani who runs Asentiv in Central India from Mumbai.

They have a process called ECC (Emotionally Charged Connection) which helped me identify my connection with my business.

I would strongly recommend this for business owners for them to find their ECC.

Now, it's your turn my friend and if you have been reading so far, then you must have already realised that this book is not only about reading, but working on it. If you have done the exercise in the chapter above, you should know your basic why by now.

I hope you also find a story that connects you with your business. This story helps you talk about your why to more people. I assure you that we are going to help you with this in the coming chapters so that you would be able to communicate *"your why"* to the world.

Simply put, by now you should be knowing *"why are you doing what you are doing right now"?*

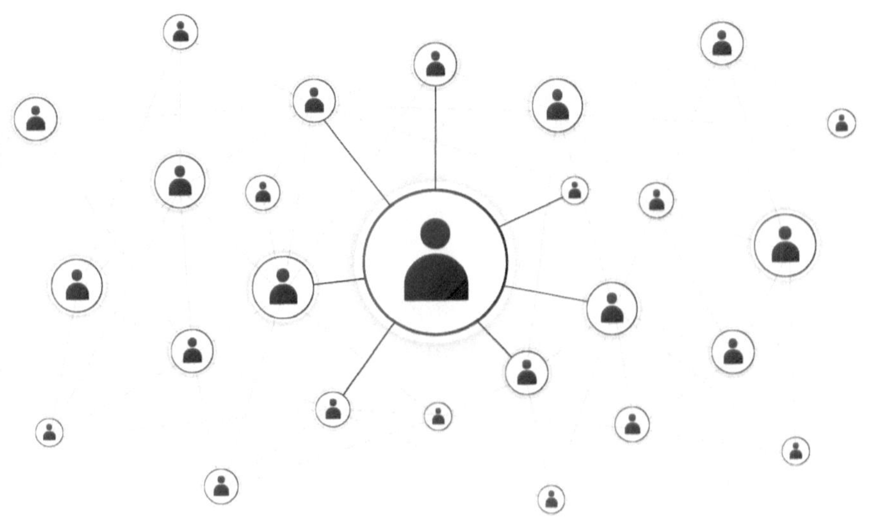

CHAPTER
Two

How to use your "why" to connect to people? (Vision)

HAVE YOU FOUND YOUR WHY?

Now that you have found your why, it's time to tell it to the world too!

So, why would you want to tell your why to other people?

Well, more often than not, I have found that - "people only join your cause when YOU have one."

Your why is like your cause and the reason for "why you are doing what you are doing".

If you have not found it till now, it is something you will be doing eventually because that will fulfil you and make you feel worthwhile.

So, how will you use your why to connect with people?

You can make it a part of your "Vision" and share it with people who will help you to share it further easily.

We know that companies have a vision, but so should each one of us.

One day, if you sit down and decide what all you want to achieve for this vision of your life, this will definitely help you.

You can get a lot of online resources to help you with this and some of the ones who helped me were

1. "Vishen Lakhiani (Mindvalley)"'s three important questions is a very different way of finding your vision quickly.

Vishen says that we should think of our goals in 2 ways which are Means Goals and End Goals. We should know our End goals and list them down as this will attract them in our lives and also help us get to them.

In fact, there is a complete video which can guide you to do that and you can find that on youtube at the link - http://youtu.be/f8eU5Pc-yog or just by searching for the 3 most important questions by Vishen Lakhiani.

You can find a copy of his document that he recommends to do this exercise at the end of this book in the appendices as Appendix 1

2. Visioning Workshops - I was also fortunate to attend a workshop by Lois Weinblatt. A one day workshop with Lois helped me set 360-degree goals for my life and as a result, I designed one page of vision which reminds me where I want to go. You can get further details of this workshop at True North Visionaries website.

3. Vision Boards - People also recommend Vision Boards which help remind you every day of why you are doing what you are doing.

A vision board is a creative process to set clear intentions and goals for what you want in your life, so you can grow and transform yourself.

The secret behind why a vision board works is the idea to attract what you truly want, but You must see it, feel it, and embody it.

There are four essential steps to make a vision board:

A. Defining your goals
B. Finding your inspiration
C. Mapping out your board
D. Displaying your vision board

You can get more details of this technique to find your visions through many classes and also online tools available.

You can use any of these techniques to help you find and set your visions and find out for yourself, so when you connect the same to your business, it might help you find your why for your business also.

THE OTHER WAY TO DISCUSS YOUR WHY -

The other way to discuss your "why" is with stories like I did in chapter one, where I connected my life events with my "why". This helped me realise why I like doing what I am doing right now.

DO YOU KNOW WHOM YOU ARE SPEAKING TOO?

The next step, when you get your vision or connection of your why of your business, is to talk about it to people.

This book aims to connect you with others through your life story. So all you have to do is that you have to speak to people. However, all people are not the same and there are different people who have different styles of connecting with people. Every person has a different personality type and their lots of theories available to analyse and differentiate people into various types.

Without going into complexities about the same, our purpose is to connect to the person we are talking to and to communicate our "why" to them.

Relating to this, I think of people in 2 behavioural aspects:

Are they emotional?

Are they analytical?

These are the 2 types of people who understand our "why" differently.

For example, some of you would have connected more to the second story of my grandfather as that was based on emotions and was less factual.

The ones who would have been analytical would have connected with the story of the facts relating to the business owners having a lonely journey as it was more fact-based with events unfolding and more highlighted facts.

WHY ARE TELLING STORIES IMPORTANT TO COMMUNICATE OUR "WHY"?

Some of you must have figured out by now that the best way to communicate your why is through "the story of your life."

There are many reasons for that and the foremost reason is that what connects with us on an emotional basis is what stays with us, and we can remember it for a longer time.

Think about it, all of us remember the stories that our grandmother or mother told us as a child but do we remember any discussions as clearly as the stories? Maybe, you might remember a few factual discussions which are etched in your memory, but stories surely help connect faster and have a deeper impact on our minds.

In short, the saying *"Facts Tell, but Stories Sell"* is so true.

REFINING YOUR STORY (DIFFERENT STORIES FOR DIFFERENT OCCASIONS AND PEOPLE)

With the help of my book, I want to help you find your story now.

I would like you to remember events from your past right now.

Try to remember the incidents which you can recollect at this moment, and I will be helping you to remember around 3 of them below.

The idea is to just remember the incident with the help of the small pointers given below. Not the complete story but something that is of strong emotional value and is deeply embedded in your memory.

The emotions do not have to be only pleasant incidents; they can be sad, angry or terrible moments or maybe feelings of loneliness etc.

They can also be happy and pleasurable moments which are like the *"wow moments"* of your life.

How about moments of extreme joy, surprise, excitement or any winning moment?

Time to write the 3 most significant moments of your life

....

....

1. ....

....

....

....

....

2. ....

....

....

....

....

3. ....

....

....

....

....

Now ask yourself, What does that make you feel?

Moment 1 - Feeling

....

....

....

....

Why does it make you feel like that?

What do you want to do today, with that feeling?

Did the answers connect with your "why" today?

If Yes, how? (If no, maybe this is not the reason for your "why" for today.)

Moment 2 - Feeling

Why does it make you feel like that?

What do you want to do today, with that feeling?

....

....

....

....

Does this connect with your "WHY" today? If Yes, how? (If no, maybe this is not the reason for your "why" today.)

....

....

....

....

Moment 3 - Feeling

....

....

....

Why does it make you feel like that?

....

....

....

....

What do you want to do today with that feeling?

....

....

....

....

Does this connect with your "why" today? If Yes, how? (If no, maybe this is not the reason for your "WHY" today.)

....

....

....

....

I hope that by now, you would have connected to at least 1 moment to your "why".

This is how you get started and in the times to come, you will start getting other moments in your memory and will be able to easily find more moments connected with your "why".

Once you have got the moments identified, relive those moments again and write down the complete story as you can recollect it along with your feelings of what you were going through.

Also, think why you feel strongly about this?

How does this affect what you do today?

And with this, you would have found the story of your life.

These stories will help you connect with all the people who come into your life and are significant to you.

Some of them will share your thoughts and some will identify themselves with you easily.

They will be ready to help you with your "why" and to make your vision come true.

I would also strongly like to recommend you to enrol yourself in a proper course with Asentiv and learn their ECC technique (Emotionally Charged Connection technique) to find your story and connect it with your business.

There are many other such techniques available including psycho-geometrics, business story telling courses and so please do find one and take it.

This will help you connect your "why" with your inner self and your life events which not only makes it believable for others but easy for them to relate too.

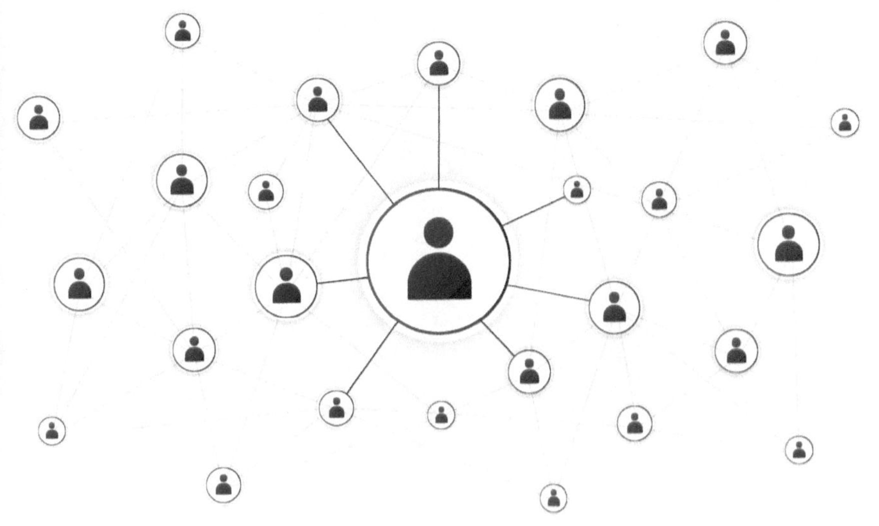

CHAPTER
Three

What is your business? (Value)

YOUR BUSINESS IS NOT WHAT YOU DO.....

Some of you must be wondering what this means and so please do read on and I hope to be proved right…

By now, you know your **"why"** and at least one story of "why you do what you do".

Also, you know, how your story connects with what you are as a person and how you want to make a difference around you and in you.

If you have a business, then the easiest way to make this difference is through your business and we discovered this with the **"6 why techniques"** in chapter 1.

However, for some of you, it might still not have been easy to connect with the idea immediately.

The idea of this book is to slowly draw you into how you can tell your story to the world and so it's time to dig deeper into your business.

What is your business?

....

....

....

....

When we ask this question to so many people, the answer is almost the same and can be boring as they reply just in terms of a noun. I am an architect; I am a CA, I am…...

It does not require the other person wanting to know more as you have answered the question to end the conversation instead of starting one.

Now some of you must be thinking that how else can we answer that question as our business is what we have just said.

You are right as we have not thought about it in another manner as yet and so let's think about it from one another way….

ALL BUSINESSES EXIST TO ADD VALUE (SOLUTION).

I am sure that all of you own a car, or you will own one soon?

If not, let it be as simple as that you must have used a car or a vehicle at one point of your life.

Why do you own a car or why have used a vehicle?

Right now let's not speak about "A particular type of car" but just a car.

I think you must have answered that with - to commute from one place to another.

Let's say the reason can be that you want to reach your destination easily and quickly. (Though I am not sure if this is possible in our cities in India right now with all the traffic and chaos on the roads.)

How many of you bought the car just to keep it parked in your garage? (once again think of your first car even if you have that Rolls Royce or Bentley parked in the garage to be taken out only for those special occasions when needed).

So, primarily the need for the car was to answer your need for moving from one place to another.

Each product or service that we buy adds some value in our life.

It is often said that *"we do not buy a drill, but we buy the hole that is needed to hang a painting or put a shelf or whatever the hole is required for; which is why we buy the drill." This means that the drill is only the means but what we need is the hole (that is what the drill gives to us as the value)*

This applies to everything that you have bought for your personal needs or for your business needs.

For your personal needs, everything you bought was to satisfy your requirements of

- Comfort (Basic Physiological needs)
- Safety (Need to feel safe)
- Show Off (For getting attention from other people, for love and connection or belongingness or for needs of esteem)
- Feeling Good/Fulfilled (When we give a donation without our name attached or if we even give some food/clothes to another person without expecting anything or even our name. Or when we go out of the way for someone even when there is nothing in return)

MASLOW'S PYRAMID OF HIERARCHY OF NEEDS

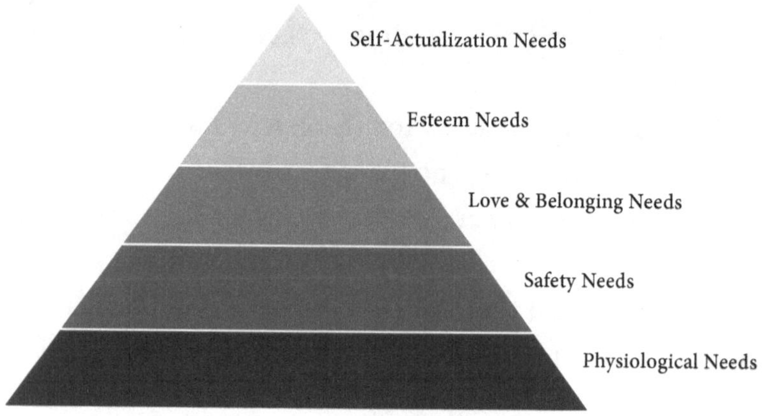

This concept is depicted above. The Maslow's Pyramid is a way to depict the Maslow's Hierarchy of Needs, which is a theory in psychology proposed by Abraham Maslow in 1943.

I am using it here more to depict the reason a person might be buying your product or services and not as yet to position it as a hierarchy.

It is Easier Why it Comes to Buying for a Business.

The best part is that it is easier if your products or services are connected with business needs as basically there are only 2 basic needs:

To Save Money
or
To Make Money

Some people say that in business, sometimes they are supplying a service which is to run the business and my submission is, even that is to make more money by becoming more efficient.

Is that not why personal assistants (Typists) got replaced by the trusted computer?

FIND OUT HOW YOU ADD VALUE

So, the only reason you have a business is because you satisfy some need.

This need is the "**Value**" that you provide, where others are ready to exchange another value in terms of currency to get the value your product gives to them.

It is time to get to work.....

What value do you provide?

....

....

....

....

If your business provides a service or product to their business owners, all you have to do is think about it in only 2 questions...

How does your product or service help other business owners save money?

....

....

....

....

OR

How does your product or service help the other business owners make more money than he already does so now?

....

....

....

....

If you can answer even any one of these questions, you have found what value you provide to others.

Now, If your product is for individual consumers, you might have to think about these questions below...

STEP 1 is an easy step to find out what value does your product or service add to the person purchasing it?

Another way to ask this can be:-
"What does the customer get after buying your product or service?

- Car – Ease of reaching a place
- Clothes – Protection for the body
- Dentist – Cure to toothache (the first thing in the mind) or a Beautiful smile
- Pen – To write on paper
- Drill – a hole
- (your product) – (the value you give)

What value do you provide as a business owner?

....

....

....

....

The above would be a good place to start and end and leave it at that for your first communication with most everyone.

However, we have gone down the path of Maslow, so some of you could also consider going into this a little deeper to be able to use it later if needed.

STEP 2 - Let's try and find out where and through which need, your product fits in the Maslow Pyramid that we discussed above.

I request you to try to mention it here and answer:-

What need does your product meet in Maslow's Pyramid?

....

....

....

....

You will have to then answer the following questions.

Are your products cheaper than the other products and services available, or are they equally priced?

If your answer is no and you are more expensive, then which other needs are you offering from the above pyramid of needs?

....

....

....

....

Let me ask you to consider this with an example,

Consider the earlier example of the Rolls Royce, it satisfies the need for travel but also takes care of esteem needs.

One must consider and decide which is the bigger need that it supplies over here?

So if your product is also figured out in 2 segments of needs, you have to define which segment overpowers the others when you want to find the value you provide.

Though you might speak about the other need, your emphasis should be on the overpowering need that your product or service meets.

Now, this is not that easy as we might think that a higher need for esteem is the best way to make the most profits.

This need has to be in the mind of the buyer and not us, as *THEY* define whether you are fulfilling that need. Therefore, you might need to keep finding out your value.

In this book, our job is to help you to talk about your business and connect with other people. Let us not forget that, and so at this stage, it is important to find the value your product or service adds to the life of the person ready to exchange value for it.

THE VALUE OF TESTIMONIALS

The value is what your business is about, in other words, testimonials given by your clients.

Your business is, therefore, *not what you do but how it adds value to the person* who is using your product or service. It's what your customer gets after he has bought the product or service from you.

If you can start talking about this when you communicate with your prospects and customers, you will find that your value proposition is what will drive you and your business.

Here is where it gets tricky as it's not as easy as defining our value.

Your best guides for this exercise could be to ask your very own customers why they do business with you as that will also add to your business story.

And now, your next exercise is to call up 3 customers and ask them these simple questions:

Customer 1

Question 1 - Why do you do business with me?

....

....

....

....

Question 2 - How does my product or service add value to your life/business?

....

....

....

....

Question 3 - Why do you choose me above my other competitors?

....

....

....

....

Customer 2

Question 1 - Why do you do business with me?

....

....

....

....

Question 2 - How does my product or service add value to your life/business?

....

....

....

....

Question 3 - Why do you choose me above my other competitors?

....

....

....

....

Customer 3

Question 1 - Why do you do business with me?

....

....

....

....

Question 2 - How does my product or service add value to your life/business?

....

....

....

....

Question 3 - Why do you choose me above my other competitors?

....

....

....

....

The idea is to find the value that you offer them, and which is the reason they are buying from you.

Whatever input they give you, try to dig down a little deeper to understand the reason so that you know what is that important part of your business that makes people come to you to use the products or services you offer.

WHAT MAKES YOU A "SPECIALIST"?

Let's try and summarise what you must have found with listing it below:

1. What are they buying from you?

....

....

....

2. Why are they buying it?

....

....

....

3. Why do they choose you above your competitors?

....

....

....

The days of being generalists are soon fading as the online market has come to capture our business.

Earlier only products were being sold online, but these days even other services are being offered online with the ever-increasing internet speeds for e.g. video calling is becoming more common, online medical consultations is already a reality and the online services world is developing faster.

To combat this, you will have to become a "specialist" in your business.

You could be doing a couple of things in your business or maybe running a couple of business verticals right now, but can you say that there is that one thing that you do, that no one is better at, than you.

Also why and how can you claim that?

My favourite example to depict this is how we pick a doctor and how much do we pay?

So, let's say you had a headache very frequently since the past week,

What would you do after trying all the home remedies?

Go to a doctor and maybe to a physician. What would you pay for the consultation? Maybe Rs. 100/- to Rs 150/- (INR) in India

Now if the general physician referred you to an eye doctor, what would the consultation cost you? Around Rs. 400 to 600/- (INR) in India

If the same eye doctor said that you had to visit a cornea specialist, the consultation could cost you around Rs. 1000/- (INR) or even more.

The specialists make more money and are treated as specialists and also get more respect.

We started this chapter with the idea of not saying a noun when someone asks you what do you do as the noun just signifies that you are one of many.

But if you answer this question with the value of what you do with you being a specialist, that would be the way people start connecting with you and want to know more about you and we shall move this ahead in the coming chapter.

Hopefully, you have the basic answers to the basic but very important questions so that we can move ahead to the next chapter to bring it all together.

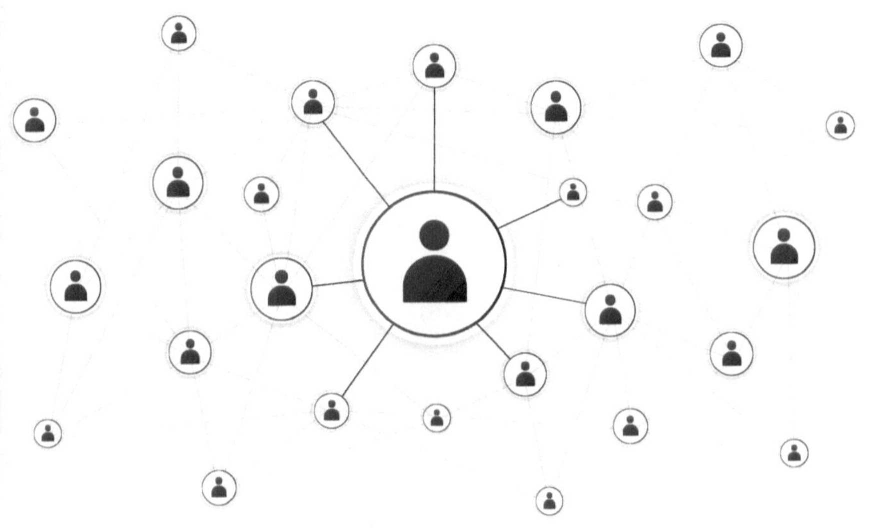

CHAPTER
Four

How to communicate about your business to others

I must congratulate you for coming so far with me through this book.

If you have reached here and if you have been working along with the small exercises that were outlined in the previous chapters of the book, you would have also found the reason for doing the business you do and also what kind of service your business provides.

It's time to start bringing this together now so that it can be used by you to help you reach the success you deserve.

YOUR VALUE STATEMENT

Please do not confuse "your value statement" with the vision statement or mission statement that different businesses put on their walls as it is an entirely different idea that we are looking for over here.

"*The Value statement*" is the value you provide to your customers that no-one else can.

Another way of putting it can be, that it is what the customer is left with, after your dealing with him has got over.

Based on the above answers that you got in the earlier two chapters, I need you to answer this question again:

What do you do? *(in the last chapter we worked on this and the value you give will go here)*

....

....

....

....

(This is Your Value Statement)
And you will end it by saying the noun that I am a

....

....

....

....

STOP BEING THE BORING "BUSINESS OWNER."

When you start your answer with a value statement, the person in front of you gets surprised to receive a different answer which helps him see value in you.

Instead of stopping the conversation, now our value statement can be a conversation starter and helps in getting you that important next meeting where he gives you a chance to explain more about your business.

This is most useful when you are networking and you meet a lot of people in one day at an event as you keep showing yourself off as an "expert" or a "Specialist" in your field.

This helps people remember you even after the meeting is over. In fact, even if some days later, when someone tells them that they are having a problem that you had told them that you could solve, they will surely remember you. This will help bring your name up as a recommendation. Even the person who is being told about you wants to deal with you, because you have been recommended and we all want to work with specialists and experts in our businesses.

You have now moved away from being that 'business owner' to a **"*solution provider*"** and who the whole world needs is a solution provider when they have a problem.

The starting point of any business transaction is when someone needs a solution. This is simple economics of needs and wants or in other words, demand and supply.

In fact, this helps them also speak about you to other people as even they want to now show off that they know someone who can help solve the problems of the people they know and that is how your reach multiple people.

LISTENING IS THE FIRST STEP IN COMMUNICATING.

Now, it's time to start strengthening your post-introductions and also your introductions at times.

A lot of you must be doing multiple things or offering many products/services which are needed by different people and for different reasons.

This means that you must be having a larger market who needs one type of solution from the many products that you might be offering and so let us try and work through that.

Now how do you know that all the work you have

done till now of making your value statement and finding more about yourself and your business can be made more effective,

And also to know if your value statement connects with the person you are talking to.

You must also be wondering as to how do you connect with one value statement with all the different kinds of people and all their different needs?

Let us try and now sort this question -

I am sure that you must have met an insurance or financial products sales-person.

He must have offered you a different range of products for example:- children's education, protection of your family on your untimely demise, products for saving funds for your retirement or for other financial goals in life.

In years of observing and having spoken to many such people involved in the marketing of financial products, I noticed one simple difference between the salesperson and the super salesperson.

In fact, this applies to most of the best salespeople in the world, no matter what they are selling.

Most salespeople admitted that they worked with a prepared script that they have spent the time to build and be perfect at.

The keyword here is "SCRIPTS". *Not one script but multiple scripts.*

When I asked them as to why they have multiple

scripts - they had a very simple one-line answer - different people have different needs and the script should be able to help them with their specific needs.

The key lies in the art of listening and understanding the need.

Accordingly, the right and the required script needs to be brought out so that you connect with your client.

Now you must be wondering how this connects with what we have covered till now or how to introduce yourself?

The answer is that this is how you become perfect at people wanting to know who you are and stay connected with you.

So, step one for any conversation is first to ask many questions and listen to what they are saying.

Some of the questions you could pick from are -

1. What do you do?
2. That sounds exciting or interesting, would love to know more about your work. How is the industry doing?
3. Where do you think would be the best scope for your business this year?
4. What are the challenges in your industry?
5. Where do you get most of your customers from? (to business owners)
6. Could I connect you to someone who could be of help to you for your business in case if I met someone? (Normally the second last question in any conversation)

7. What kind of people would those be where I could connect you?

8. Would love to know what is the goal of your company or your vision?

Another way of knowing more about the person you are speaking to.

There is one more technique of understanding the person you are dealing with and this is to do with ascertaining their listening and attention styles.

They are also known as the three different styles of learning or how we gather information around us.

The three basic types of how people gather information around them or learn about new things are in these 3 styles.

They are **visual, auditory, and kinesthetic**.

To learn anything and process the information around us, we depend on our senses.

Most people tend to use only one of their senses more than others.

This is actually a **NLP technique** also called NLP sensory vocabulary listing.

NLP shows you how to identify what the other person's behaviour is and how should you communicate with him with this simple table -

4 WAYS TO IDENTIFY HOW OTHERS GATHER INFORMATION			
Check their	**Visually Inclined People**	**Kinesthetic Inclined People**	**Auditory Inclined People**
Eye Movement While listening to you	They would be looking upright	They would normally be looking on the downright	They would look at you straight
Breathing Speed while listening to you	You can hardly see them breathing in a normal state as they only breathe through the nose	When they breathe, their tummies also move	Normally their shoulders would be moving in normal breathing
Speed of Talking when they speak to you	Normally they talk fast but are coherent	They talk slowly as they feel every word	They talk fast too but sometimes lose their track and become incoherent also.

Now that you have identified as to what style of people they are and how they are inclined, you know how to speak to them better with the table below -

HOW TO SPEAK TO THEM SO THAT THEY UNDERSTAND YOU BETTER			
The language you should use	**For Visually Inclined People**	**For Kinesthetic Inclined People**	**For Auditory Inclined People**
	Use more visual words or pictorial words. Words related to sight indicate colours, shape, or appearance. For instance: gloomy, dazzling, bright, foggy, gigantic. Phrases like as bright as the sun, It was so foggy that you could not see your hand in front of you, etc.	You will need to use more touchy-feely words or action words. Words like active, affected, bearable, callous, charge, concrete, emotional, Phrases like I feel or felt like this, I had emotions like, etc.	You have to use more auditory words. Words like sound, hear, discuss, interview, listen, loud, remark, rumour, say, speechless, tune in and phrases like clear as a bell, sounds like, tune into, bells ringing, keynote speaker, the power of speech, purrs like a kitten, to tell you the truth, word for word.

YOUR ARSENAL IS IN YOUR VALUE AND WHY?

Most people, at one point of time, will ask you what you do?

Every time someone asks me this, I smile in my heart as I know that I am ready as I have listened enough and I am confident I know what to speak.

Believe me, even You are ready, but you need to perfect yourself by taking out the right weapon from your arsenal of weapons.

With this technique, not only you will be able to speak to the person but also connect with them.

By now, it must be clear to you that every person connects with a person for a reason.

If the reason is business, then let me remind you again that they would like to connect with you for 2 main reasons - to make more money or to save money.

Your **"value statement"** is your weapon which helps them to bring clarity on how you can help them make more money or save more money by your work.

As you ask the questions to them, you should be forming an opinion in your head.

This you can do by actively listening to find the solution they need for helping them do better at what they are doing.

Also, you can see how you and your product/ service can fit into their requirements to help them actually do better.

The first answer to their question of what you do now

should be this "Value statement" as it adds value in their lives.

So, if you want to make sure that you get and keep their attention for as long as you need to be able to make your complete sales pitch, you should only be speaking 2 sentences which will make all the difference which does not take more than 45 seconds to a minute.

Sentence one - Value Statement ending with your business.

Sentence two - You have been able to do this by (put your biggest strength over here) for (these number of) clients amongst which the most interesting one was for (this particular client) that you would like to tell them about.

STORIES WILL HELP THEM REMEMBER YOU AFTER YOU LEFT THEM.

So far, we have covered in this chapter that when you meet someone for the first time, you have to ensure that if you want to make this a meaningful connection, you need to follow the given two steps.

Step 1 is about questioning them and uncovering their needs and knowing what could be stopping them.

Step 2 is about giving them 2 statements only about what you do with your value statement and that you have a story about this.

Time to take the next step and that is to be able to tell your story and you should make a decision whether you should do it over there or ask for a special appointment where you can narrate your story.

The best way which works here is to just tell the synopsis of the story over there is only a minute or two.

Then you can ask for an appointment to be able to tell more details of the story if they are interested and also to learn more about the other person's business.

This brings us to one of the most important parts of the next step, i.e. "Telling Stories."

This book has been trying to help you find your business story also.

Usually, there are many types of stories, but for making it easy and for the purpose of this book, there are two types of stories which you should have made by now:-

Stories about why you do what you do?

This helps a person to connect with you and why you are in your line of work.

Even though at times it feels that you might be sharing some personal details, you will need to do so if you want to build strong relationships with your connections.

We have covered this in chapter 1 and 2 itself. Such stories can be told to everyone connected with you. They are not necessarily only for your prospective clients but also could be for your suppliers, financiers and partners or stakeholders too.

Stories about your "Value statement."

These are normally the stories that help your customer connect with what you are offering by understanding the value of doing business with you.

The format of the story should go something like this.

- What was the problem being faced?
- How was it getting worse and what could it lead to?
- Where and when did you meet and how did the conversation go?
- What was your action plan?
- How did this lead to a solution which was beneficial for the person in front?

This is also called the problem-solution method.

It is time to try your hand at such a kind of story, so let's try and help you find 3 stories for you. These could also be an extension of the work that you did in chapter 3 when you asked your clients about question no 3 asking them as to why they chose to work with you.

STORY NO 1

ValueStatement:

....

....

....

What was a problem being faced by the client?

....

....

....

If nothing was done, what would happen?

(dramatise the details, but please do not make it unbelievable. On the other hand, do not agree to say not much would have happened)

....

....

....

How and where did you meet the client?

(You could make this part funny and entertaining also. Actually, this is the only part where you can be funny)

....

....

....

How did you solve the problem?

(include your action plan with some details without being completely technical as the time for that will come when they invite you to give a proposal later)

....

....

....

What was the end result?

(This should always be connected with actual results and the feelings of the customer and not only one part of it)

STORY NO 2

ValueStatement:

....

....

....

What was the problem being faced by the client?

....

....

....

If nothing was done, what would happen?

(dramatise it but please do not make it unbelievable. On the other hand, please also do not agree to say not much would have happened)

....

....

....

How and where did you meet the client?

(You could make this part funny and entertaining also. Actually the only part from all the 5 parts)

....

....

....

How did you solve the problem?

(what did you do with some details without being completely technical as the time for that will come when they invite you to give a proposal later)

....

....

....

What was the end result?

(This should always be connected with actual results and the feeling of the customer in front both and not only one part of it)

STORY NO 3

ValueStatement:

....

....

....

What was a problem being faced by the client?

....

....

....

If nothing was done then what would happen?

(dramatise it but please do not make it unbelievable. On the other hand, please also do not agree to say not much would have happened)

....

....

....

How and where did you meet the client?

(You could make this part funny and entertaining also)

....

....

....

How did you solve the problem?

(explain the solution with some details without being completely technical as the time for that will come when they invite you to give a proposal letter)

....

....

....

What was the end result?

(This should always be connected with actual results and the feeling of the customer and not only one part of it)

If you do the exercises given above, you have all your weapons ready to achieve more out of your business or professional conversations.

Now your Initial first introductions will open more doors for you to make your business pitches and share more about your products or solutions.

I would like to end this part of the book by wanting to give you very important guidance.

When you start using this system of speaking, at first, it will seem odd to you and there will be times when you will also get lost in the conversation as you will not be natural at speaking in this manner at first when you start changing.

I have been using this system for the past 15 years. Even I make mistakes at times. I still sometimes misunderstand the kind of person I am talking to. Sometimes, I get too involved in my own story and completely misread the person I am speaking too. In short, let me admit that I end up telling the wrong story or bringing out the wrong value to the wrong person at times.

But as I kept practising, this became easier and easier to execute. With time and practice, the failure rates dropped from 1 in 10 to 1 in 50. I keep improving at this system of speaking for the last 15 years with the practice. More importantly, I am also able to catch myself going wrong and change my tracks in time in some conversations.

Till now, even I keep learning newer elements and so will you.

The main aim is to improve your approach of speaking to others for your work so that it becomes more effective in being able to get you the most deserving success.

So keep practising and with time, you will find that your "Value Statements" will become even more powerful. Your stories and discussion around your business will start becoming easier and your meetings will be even more successful.

In the end, it is about being able to communicate what you are and what you do, in such a compelling manner that a person feels the need to know you and wants to work with you and even recommend you when needed!

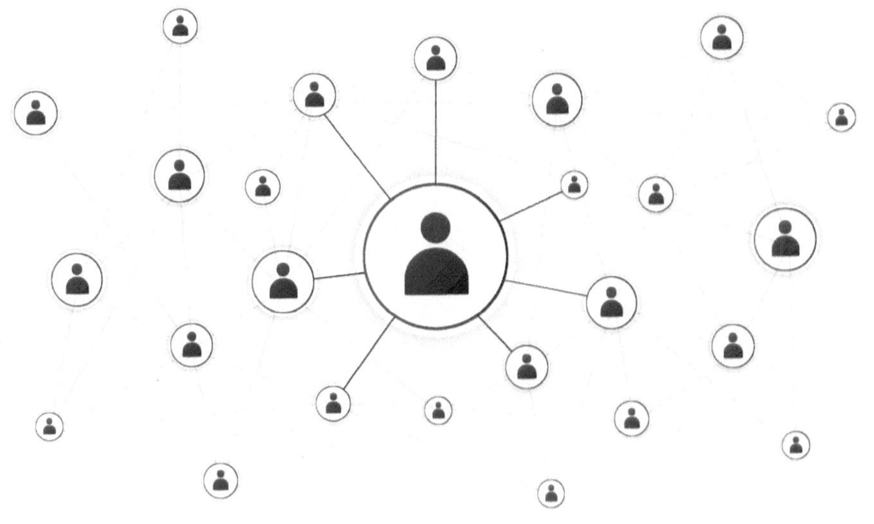

CHAPTER

Five

Where do you want to go?

IT IS NOT ENOUGH TALKING ABOUT TODAY.

Congratulations!! as now you have created all the successful tools to tell your story to others.

Until now, you have done all the exercises to talk about your past journey of reaching at this point or in other words, your current position.

You have also learnt to create your own "value statement" where you show your value to your prospects/clients or other stakeholders.

It's time to get a little more depth into this to build on the current position now.

LET'S START THINKING ABOUT YOUR EXCITING FUTURE

About 5 years ago, after I had taken over the BNI business along with my partner, friend and guide Atul Joglekar, we were invited to attend an amazing workshop. I honestly feel lucky that I got a chance to learn about visioning through this workshop.

Here we learnt to articulate our vision, and Lois Weinblatt inspired me to come up with a one-page vision of where I wanted to go.

I can't share the complete details of the workshop as that is something you might have to experience for yourself.

The Program was so dynamic that Lois made me think of what I wanted to do, where I wanted to be and by what time I wanted to have that vision as a reality.

I shared my vision with my partner Atul and at night when we were together in that hotel room in Mumbai, he told me to follow my vision and he assured me that he would support me for that.

WHAT WAS MY VISION?

I wanted to be a speaker and community builder who could help others to change their lives and as a person would be able to motivate and inspire others.

At that time, I was scared to tell anyone about my vision as I felt it was conceited and seemed like I was stepping beyond my boots.

I questioned myself, "who the hell was I to imagine and want such a vision?"

Was it a vision or just a dream with no reality?

I kept preparing myself slowly on my own for trying to visualise my closeness towards my vision.

And then something changed, about 3 years back, I got a chance to speak at the BNI Global Conference and also across some other countries of BNI as a guest speaker. I also started getting invited to other places as a speaker on communication & networking to motivate and inspire business owners.

It is then I realised that I forgot one element while discussing the manner of realizing your vision.

What was this?

TELLING AS MANY PEOPLE AS YOU CAN ABOUT YOUR VISION!

I started telling everyone (who was ready to hear about it) about my vision and there have been so many people along my journey, who became partners and supporters of my vision.

And these people are helping me today also, trying to help me realise the vision that I had for the last 3 years; by speaking about me and getting me invited to various places to speak.

So, the next step after finding your story is taking it ahead and making it true for you.

We are going to discover this together in this chapter.

Step 1 of this is, of course,to know what you want to become and I hope that the exercise that you carried out with the 3 End Goals of your Life in chapter 2 can guide you for that.

I would suggest that you spend some time and energy to attend a course where you could discover your vision.

You can also attend a class or take an online class.

But this book is not about finding your vision; on the other hand, it is about how you can tell your story, once you know what you want.

Now, let us start connecting this concept with your business at this point of time.

Here is something that you might need to think about;-

1. What is the vision for your business/ work? What will you be doing?

2. Is it in the same business or are you looking to expand/ diversify/ find new opportunities or simply want to become the best in your city/state/country in what you are doing right now?

3. An easy way to think about this would be, to possibly think about where do you see yourself in your work field 5 years from now?

4. And once again it should link with your "WHY" above?

5. Now you need to frame your story of the future again with your WHY?

It might feel scary, but let me share with you how my vision which is connected with work seems like:-

It is the 1st of January 2024 and I am so proud of the life I have created.

I have been invited to speak in 20 countries in the last 12 months and am just returning from another new country which I visited for the first time.

So far, I have visited 65 countries to create communities of like-minded individuals.

I have spoken in front of 100000 people and impacted their lives to create a successful business for them. This has got me to fill up almost 3 thank you manuals of 1000 pages.

I have also been invited on radio and TV talk shows around the world to help connect with more people and help them succeed.

I just spoke to Atul the day before yesterday and I am excited about our call today evening at 6 pm. We speak every alternate day without fail as our regions of BNI are 3100+ members is creating wonderful success for our members.

This is the first part of what you have to be ready with.

PEOPLE JOIN YOU WHEN YOU HAVE A CAUSE.

Now comes the scary part, where it is not enough to have your future clear to you only, but at this point of time, you need to share it with others.

We discussed Maslow's Pyramid earlier and we also learnt that it has different levels of needs and let me show it to you over here again and try and explain how you use this to speak about your vision.

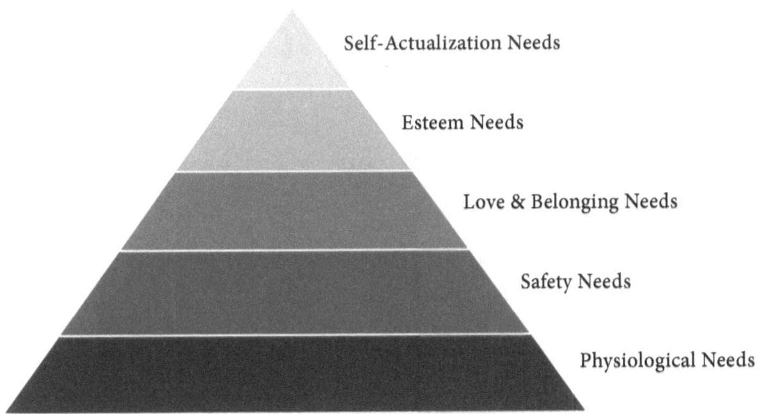

Very similarly, you will see that Our relationships with people are also at different levels:-

- **Basic Needs** - At this level, you only talk about the basics where you only speak about transactions - sales and purchases.

  This is basically how most business relationships start.

- **Safety (Need of feeling safe)** - This is where you start trusting the other person at the next level and also where people start giving credit to their buyers.

  They also want to keep the relationships safe as this provides the safety of having found a good supplier or a good client.

- **Feeling of Belonging** - If you want to take the relationship to the next level, this is where you start talking about your industry and also about what the other person wants to do.

  You may need to know how you are in the same kind of industry or in the same economic problem.

THIS IS IT!

This is the stage where you can bring in your future plans in the conversation.

You can ask for their future plans and how you can help them to achieve their plans too.

- **Esteem Needs** - This is where you need to share your vision completely with them and let them be aware of what you are planning to do and where do you see yourself in the next 5 years.

- **Feeling Good/Fulfilled** - This is the next stage and we shall speak about this in the next part of this chapter.

By now, we have understood that people join your cause only when you have one.

By this, we mean that only when people know where you want to go, can they think about helping you to reach your goal.

It is important for you to share the appropriate time of **"where you want to be"** as that will open more doors for you than you can imagine.

This is definitely not a book on philosophy, but I cannot resist adding a small thought that I have started having more and more belief in:-

"If you are sure of where you want to go, the entire universe will help you get there."

You may call it the **Law of attraction** or anything else you want too.

I like to call it **"The power of the people"** we know and who they know further.

In other words, this is also called networking and that is where we will slowly go before the book ends, but I do not want you to think about that for now.

MAKE YOUR VISION SCARY ENOUGH TO EXCITE YOU.

There is one particular level of relationships where you need to speak at another level.

Let's find out more about this.

Sometimes while setting our vision, we do not want to really stretch it as we feel that it would sound completely ridiculous.

As a result, we end up setting lower and achievable goals for ourselves.

It is completely okay if you have done that too.

But, here is my challenge to you!

Are you ready to step out of your limits in the secret place of your mind and try to think a little more out of your comfort zone?

As the founder of BNI, Dr. Ivan Misner says, *"Why accept mediocrity when excellence is an option?"*

There is a concept called -

BHAG which stands for **Big Hairy Audacious Goals**.

Though goals are very different from a vision technically, but over here, let us make it easier for you to keep it all as one.

So that you can set **SAV - Scary Audacious Vision for yourself!!**

If you get that, you will know that this was because of your vision.

I want you to think about that one moment in the future which you think will show you that you have achieved your SAV, which is one part of the complete Vision of your Life.

Let us keep this for your work achievement since this book is about your work story.

Are you ready to share your soul with yourself in the next few lines?

So take a deep breath and start answering these questions and let us see where your vision leads you....

Q 1 - Where will you be?
(please try and be as specific as you can be)
E.g., I will be on the stage of the Royal Albert Hall in London with floodlights on me after finishing a speech

....

....

(If you are going to be in a new office, how will it look? If at your new factory, where will it be situated and how big it would be?

Imagine how it will look, even from a drone?

Q 2 - What time will it be?
When will this be? (Again imagine it specifically)
E.g., It will be 6 pm in the evening on a warm summer evening in the year 2025

....

....

....

(Is it morning, is it the opening of your office, factory, shop? What will be the occasion?)

Q 2 - Who all would be there?
E.g., There would be around 5000 people who hear me address them for the complete day.

....

....

....

(How many people? Who all? Why are they there? What are they wearing?

Q-3 - What are they doing?

E.g., They are giving me a standing ovation while clapping and cheering.

....

....

....

(This might seem very illogical, but it is important as that is what makes the feelings real for you)

Q 4 - Of all the people, who is the special one over there, what is his/her expression and how is he/she feeling?

E.g., My wife Yamini is also there to encourage me there, as always. Sitting in the centre seat of the first row, she is looking around with pride on her face and love and encouragement for me.

....

....

....

Q5 - Why are the people there?

E.g., Each one of them has paid 1000 Euro to come and listen to me talk about "how to become more successful in life."

(The funny secret I will share with you is that I know they are paying a lot to hear me, but I never know whether I am receiving that payment or not! Strange thought but as they say that a mind is a funny place!)

Q 6 - What are you doing?

E.g., With my folded hands, I bow down and call my wife on stage and introduce her as that person because of whom, I am what I am today?

Q 7 - What am I feeling?

E.g., I am feeling humbled and grateful to all those who are responsible for me having reached my vision.

I am also thankful to the people in the auditorium, who are a part of my vision becoming a reality. I have tears in my eyes.

Now, I want to know from you:-

Were you able to feel my vision?

Every time I say the word "vision", my eyes shine as they are filled with tears of happiness and gratitude, while I feel and live that moment again.

Now, it's time for you to enjoy the same moment by combining all that you have written above, envisioning the future of your work....

....

....

....

....

....

You have your story ready now, to share with the relationships, reaching the last level where you are both sharing your thoughts and speaking about the future also.

SHARING YOUR SAV (SCARY AUDACIOUS VISION) IS THE ONLY WAY TO MAKE IT COME TRUE.

So you have your SAV, now what?

You might think:- Do I share this SAV with everyone? Maybe not...

You might feel uncomfortable sharing this in the beginning as you are letting people peep into your soul and read your secret thoughts.

I suggest that you start with someone whom you trust and who will listen to your SAV.

This will give you the confidence to be able to share this with more people.

They say that it takes only '1' right person for your dreams to become a reality and this is the power of sharing your SAV.

With this, people will start helping you take the required steps.

They will also help you grow to get closer to where you want to be.

Let me share one last story with you for this section:-

I was having a wonderful conversation with a young business owner whom we shall call Aditya, who was in his early 30's and was running a traditional business of construction items supply.

I thought I should share my SAV with him as he had also shared where he wanted to build his business.

I told him to make his vision so that he could have a systematic path of his needs and wants.

We parted after the conversation.

After a few days, he gave me a call and said that he might not be able to get me immediately in front of 5000 people, but he would like to introduce me to an educational institute which might help me meet many more people.

Through this, I could inspire them and help them with my knowledge.

That was my first chance to speak to students at an educational institute.

Did it help me achieve my SAV immediately?

No! But it took me one step closer to achieving it in the future!

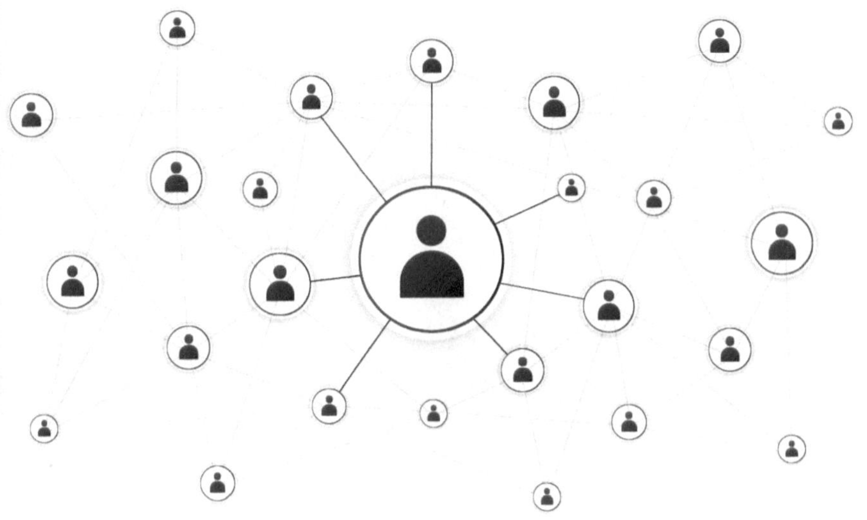

CHAPTER
Six

*Business Operator versus
Business Owner*

Congratulations to all of you, who have not only been reading this book but also working on your business and stories with the earlier chapters.

You must have made all the notes in the book itself, or some of you organised ones might be keeping a separate diary.

Even if you have not done that, I am sure that most of you must have definitely got some ideas by now, of the following things that we covered till now:

- Why are you doing what you are doing?
- How do you tell your "why" of what you are doing to others?
- How to speak to others about your business?
- You should have got your SAV (Scary Audacious vision)

This is your tool kit to start connecting with people!

It's time now to change track and go to the other important part of this book.

This is about not only telling your story but making your story come true!!

I was once asked a commonly asked question from two of my friends who are fantastic trainers. They are Mr. Murali Sundaram who is also known as the happiness coach and Mr. KVT Ramesh, the founder of Pick a Book. They have asked this question to a lot of other business people as well:

Are you a Business Owner or a Business Operator?

The first time I heard this question, I got surprised and it hit me like a stone on my head and I needed time to understand the implications of this thought.

This chapter is all about this thought and the transition from becoming a business operator to a business owner.

IS YOUR BUSINESS CURRENTLY MATCHING YOUR GROWTH PLANS?

Most of us start our business from scratch; if you are a first-generation business owner, we have to start with handling every part of our business personally.

If you start doing well, your business starts growing and you have more to handle and this keeps happening till we reach what is called our level of incompetence.

We handle so many things and at one point of time, we cannot handle anything more.

This is when this question becomes the most important question.

My partner Atul and I started the BNI business together and we loved the part of the business where we could actually speak with our BNI members and eventually help them succeed through networking.

I just loved the idea of making each member discover

their journey from the many learnings that I have shared in this book in the earlier chapters. Every time there was some success for our members, I got the inspiration to work harder than before.

We started off with 147 members who were a part of 5 chapters (each group in BNI is known as a chapter) in our BNI regions.

We managed to expand it even before we took over the business and after 1 year, we were close to 333 members and 9 chapters.

Due to this expansion, we kept getting busier and busier.

But the success and happiness of seeing entrepreneurs succeed kept feeding our souls and we were fuelled to do more.

By the end of the first year in business, we had close to 500 members with 13 chapters and it became a real business.

We got national and international success as we were called to be the speakers and leaders across BNI In India.

I was nominated by an international body called the "Founders Circle" and invited to speak abroad.

At one point, when we got the time to sit down and speak, we realised that not only were we reaching our level of incompetence but even our level of control and we would stop growing if we did not let go.

We had 2 choices -

1. Get more time and energy

2. Stop doing the work we knew could be done by others.

That is when we started building a team aggressively and started sharing the cause of doing BNI to others.

I have a saying which I keep repeating –

People join your cause only when you have one and they know what it is.

We got a team of other entrepreneurs wanting to join us. They wanted to make a difference in other business owners' lives. Like us, they were ready to give the time and energy to help other business owners to succeed.

I know that we shall be grateful to so many of them who believed in our vision and joined us to make a difference in other business owners' lives.

That helped us scale up the business or actually double our region to 20 chapters and 1000+ members in another 2 years or so.

I am not sure if my story resonated with you or not.

You might think that you do not have any surplus time and moreover, how can you think about taking the next leap for your business?

Please take the leap of faith and spend money on building your team of employees and start spending more time only growing rather than working in your business.

Stop operating your business and start owning it.

CAPACITY TO GROW

Now some of you must have reached that part also and would be thinking that I have an office which works by itself.

I am not sure, but if you have set your Scary Audacious Goal (SAV) then have you seen which activities let you take a step closer to what you want to become in your life?

Let me try and explain this by continuing my story shared above:-

So now, we had built a team and we were doing well.

We kept growing and were the best performing BNI Regions in the world.

And once again, we reached the level of incompetence!

Or probably, our goals just became bigger and without knowing it, we started following our vision.

Our team was helping us and we were doing okay.

But we had not created a capacity to keep growing.

At that time, we were lucky to attend a workshop organised by BNI and at the cost of repeating myself, will mention it again as it is part of this episode.

There was this lady whom I had referred to earlier called Ms. Lois Weinblatt; she took us on a day-long journey to make our vision.

That is when we found what we wanted to do and I also found my Scary Auditious Vision (SAV).

When you know what you want to do, it's almost as if new paths start opening out in front of you, call it The *Law of Attraction* or whatever you may.

Atul got the role of heading India and that was just fantastic.

I was being invited to train across the world and I started inspiring and motivating more leaders and business owners.

And that is where I had to learn my next lesson, as in spite of opportunities, and in an abundance of the possibilities to do more, the paths started becoming more unclear and roads kept getting blocked.

Our business in BNI also became stagnant and it was time to learn another lesson.

We had not built the capacity to grow to the level of what we had in mind.

Since then, we have done things differently and it is too early to tell this part of the story, but we are now again building the capacity to grow.

This gives us the time to start following our Vision and our SAV again.

ARE YOU WORKING FOR TODAY OR FOR TOMORROW?

The question for you to consider now is :

Is what you are doing today going to lead you to your vision tomorrow?

If the answer is no, then it is the best thing that you know now.

Why do I say that?

You have now got onto the first step that you know where you have to start.

Define where you want to go?

Now do an audit of your daily schedule, describing what you do on a daily basis, how you use your time and energy?

Now, give up those parts that do not help you reach closer to your vision.

One of the techniques that I learnt in this was the 168 hours planner.

WHAT IS A 168 HOURS PLANNER?

There are 168 hours in every week and how you use those hours, will determine if you are using it to reach closer to your goals or are you going further from it.

By using the 168 hours planner, you can find out how you are spending this time and is there any way of optimising your time and using it to do more to achieve your vision of your life.

We can also think about it in a way where we could divide our time into 3 buckets as shown in the diagram below and how do you manage these buckets.

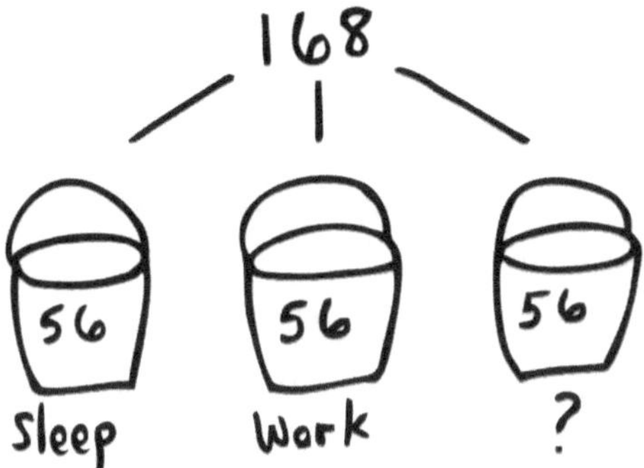

This is the most common way in which we use our time:

56 hours a week in rest/sleep at 8 hours a day.

56 hours a day in work at 8 hours a day though we know that most of us entrepreneurs actually spend more time than that on work.

The other 56 hours are for daily needs, family time, leisure, etc.

The 2 most important parts of this are:

1.   Can you control the last bucket of 56 hours?

2.   Which part of your business are you using your work bucket for?

Now how do you move ahead?

Step 1   use the 168 hours in appendix 2 of the book and see how you use your time.

Step 2   From the work time, please make a list of the work which is possible for you to delegate with your existing team.

Step 3   Find out how much time can you make free?
Is this enough to start pursuing your goals? If not, go to step 4

Step 4   For which sets of activities, do you need to hire people?

Step 5   Find out how much time can you make free now? Is this enough for you to start pursuing your goals along with the time you freed up from the above time?

Step 6 If this is still not enough, maybe you need to examine if your current business allows you to scale up, or is it getting in between your work.

Also, have a look right at the start of chapter 1 for further clarification.

5 LEVELS OF ENTREPRENEURSHIP

Don't let your today come in the way of your tomorrow.

My father worked for the Birla group almost 30 years back and he used to tell me that one of the ways the Top Manager or Profit heads of any Birla Profit centre was judged was as to how much free time did he have in a day?

It was because they knew that if the person does not have any free time to think of the expansion of new ideas or for meeting the right people to act upon the business, then they were paying the person as a business operator and not the business owner.

That system might have changed now, but the idea behind it was sound and is even more important for a business owner or an individual, especially today.

Climb the journey of becoming an entrepreneur

I heard about this concept when I was first invited to a seminar by Mr Sanjay Chaturvedi, the then CEO for Action Coach India.

Here he quoted the founder of Action Coach, Brad sugars on the 5 levels of entrepreneurship and you can find his talks on Youtube also.

According to Brad Sugars and the Action Coach Team, the 5 levels of entrepreneurship are as follows:

Level 1 is self-employment - This is when you start a new business and you do every function yourself from sales, purchase to operations and also be an office boy, at times.

Level 2 is the employer and manager. In this step, you start to employ a few people to work for you and you manage a small team of workers. Most of the work to grow your business is only done by you.

Level 3 of the levels of entrepreneurs is a business owner - At this level, now you have a team who is working for you and you also have different teams handling different functions. This gives you time to get out of the functions which do not add to your growth of business and you start training other people also into this role.

Level 4 is an investor - This is the phase where you start investing out of your business also as now there is a steady flow of money which is being handled by others for the day to day work.
You have time to grow your business. You can think of collaborations and strategies to leverage the next levels of growth.

Level 5 is Entrepreneurship - This can be best defined in the words of Brad Sugars only -"An entrepreneur uses other people's ideas, talent and time to create wealth."

Which level are you at, in this entrepreneurship ladder? Where do you want to be?

What will define this, will be your age, the level of energy you have along with your vision and having a clear picture of where you see yourself in 5, 10 years or even 15 years down the road.

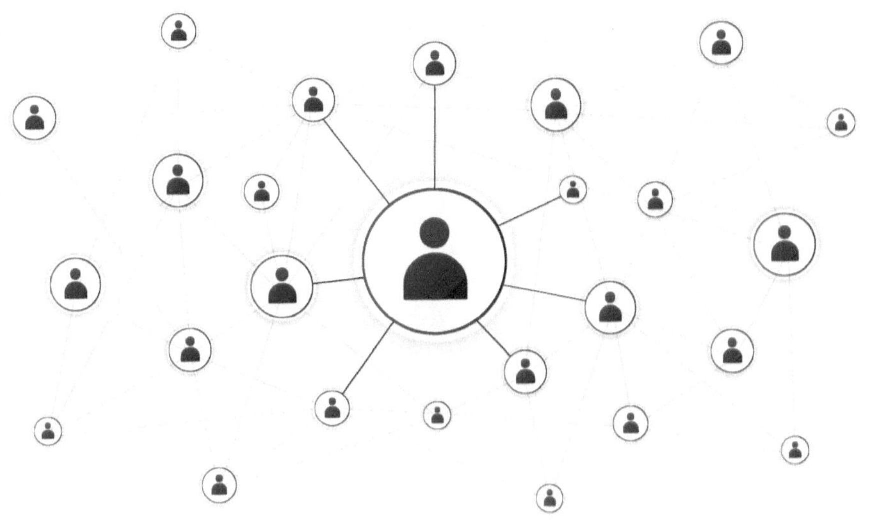

CHAPTER

Seven

Who you meet defines how you grow?

I believe that one of the reasons why I am invited to speak at many places is that they know that I have invested a lot of time and energy learning about networking.

It is the honest truth when I say that I love to see entrepreneurs succeed through networking.

There are 2 things which I am quite clear about now,

first: all the world-class business leaders know, whom they need to meet in order to achieve the next level.

second: they know what to speak to them when they get this opportunity to do so.

Till now, this book was about what you speak about yourself to achieve the goals in your life. We also made a small attempt at finding out where you want to be in the future. Now, it's important to learn how to meet the right people to achieve this success you deserve.

LONE WOLVES ARE NOT AS SUCCESSFUL AS THEY APPEAR TO BE.

Since our childhood days, we have seen movies where the main actor has a huge problem around him and then he fights his way through and comes out as a hero.

He alone is enough for many villains.

If the movie is like Singham, Dabangg or my favourite old Amitabh Bachan movies, this one person is enough!

But have you noticed that life is not like those movies?

It is a myth that all heroes are lone wolves or in other words, they alone are enough to solve their problems all alone.

Unfortunately, when we read these kinds of stories and see movies of this type, this feeling to work out our problems on our own somehow enters our mind. Also, we feel that we are weak to ask for help and support.

Similarly, the sad part of being an entrepreneur is that it is basically a lonely journey and more so, if you are a first-generation business start-up.

A business owner cannot talk about his triumphs to many people.

But it is even more scarier when there is less scope to talk about one's challenges.

Connect this with what you have learnt and acquired in your mind since childhood; it is from there only that we start trying to solve everything on our own.

I still remember the time where I had told you that I was left with fewer options at the beginning of my career and at that time I spoke about my grandfather too, but let me now fill in a few more details.

This is not to bore you with my story but to make you realise that sometimes we believe that we can work out things on our own as I did in my vain glory.

I did not appreciate the various opportunities that

were being opened up to me at that time, but sadly or luckily, things have not turned out so badly if I look at the scenario from where I stand today.

But I just increased my work only for myself!!!

I say this with all the humility that networking changed my life and so did my networks which took me another 10 to 12 years to figure out.

The idea of writing this book was to save you from many more years from this lonely journey.

At the time when I had nothing to do, 4 people helped me out.

The first one was my friend whom I had met in college and I can say that I wanted some business to work on. So, together we roamed around Gujarat and I learnt about import and exports.

We exported Atta (Flour), rice and tea and also connected with import firms who were importing Fertilisers and saw this business venture first hand.

We were amateurs and soon realised that deals were happening all around us, but our network was not strong enough to ensure that we could grow in this business at that time and thus we moved ahead instead of investing the time to build that network.

The second person who helped me was my father's friend who helped me represent him in my area for selling Floppy Diskettes and this helped me get through a few months till I found what to do where once again I moved on without building that network.

The third person was my uncle (my father's brother) who was a consumables supplier for packaging in the Pharma industry. I helped him build an entire network of pharma company who were our clients and understood how I could connect from one to another company. This was my first glimpse of networking working. Unfortunately, my uncle expired and so the industry was closed. I cannot believe it that I did not keep in touch with that complete network and let my work of connecting with people go waste.

The fourth person was my grandfather with whom, I finally joined hands with and took over the business from him. He taught me more than others, of how business was about remaining connected with people as the business was about selling and marketing.

This was finally the business which supported me to grow and find other opportunities,

We all need people around us and the sooner we accept this and start connecting with people, the faster we could reach our goals in life.

GROWTH ALWAYS NEEDS CATALYSTS (MENTORS, GUIDES AND EXPERIENCE CREATORS)

One of my favourite genres of movies is superhero movies.

Now, you must be thinking that I just said that hero-oriented movies teach us wrong myths about being a hero ourselves, here I once again exclaim that I like them.

True or not, we all like to see someone winning.

Let me tell you why.

One set of movies that I love to watch are English Superhero Movies. Now for those of you who have seen these sets of movies, there are basic 2 superhero worlds that stand out in this and they are DC Superheroes world and the Marvel Superheroes world.

DC has Superman and Wonder woman, Aquaman, Batman and such heroes who are collectively known as Justice League.

I grew up with Superman and Batman comics and thought that they were the best heroes ever.

The other world is the world of Marvel superheroes. The Marvel world of superheroes has another set of heroes like Iron man, Captain America, Hulk, Thor, Black Widow and many more who are called Avengers.

I only heard about most of these when I first saw the movies.

Logically, I should like the DC world better.

Somehow today I like the Marvel World better as a Leader as I have a reason for this.

So here is some Superhero Trivia Quiz for you?

Who is the leader of the Justice League?

Most people will easily choose Superman and if you follow that world of fiction, if Superman is dead and the others are getting beaten by the villain, it requires Superman to be brought back to life and only then can they win.

So basically, over here, the leader has to do everything and if he does not, it is the end of the world as we know it.

Time for the next question - Who is the Leader of the Avengers?

Most people would say Captain America and it might be true, when they are fighting but when I think about the person who brought them together and the person who made them come together as one team; It was Nick Fury and for me, he is the leader of the Avengers.

And think about it, which war did he fight? He had other leaders who fought to save the world, and he was at their backend and tactical support.

Superman will always remain my favourite, but I keep reminding myself that I need to be Nick Fury and have to keep surrounding myself with superheroes to do whatever is possible.

You must be wondering where I was going with this story so let me finally tell you that:

They say that growth is as much inspiration as perspiration.

You need the right people around you to start with and also who is capable of inspiring you.

You need to surround yourself with people who make you feel that it is possible to do what seems difficult for you to do.

Who is it that you have in your life whom you can speak to about your business?

How do you find such people?

I hope you are once again ready to do some exercises as this book is about having a working game-plan before we finish.

This game-plan is for you to find your success ahead.

Let's try and get an answer to the question posted above?

Who is it that you have in your life whom you can speak about for your business?

1. ....

2. ....

3. ....

Congratulations to those of you who were able to find answers.

For the others, here is some help on how to find such people for you.

Based on my experience, the following people can be a good place to start off:

- **Your friends in the business** - but if they are not in the same industry as you, it will just be general advice.

- **Another business person who deals in your industry** - that would bring more information about the industry.

- **Other businesspersons who deal with the same target market that you focus on** - this is also called a concept of contact sphere. You may have the same kind of clients, but the business is not competing with each other.

- **Your competitors** - This is difficult, but with mutual

trust and respect, if you can have your competitors as your advisors and friends, it will benefit you the most.

- **Your clients** - as they could guide you of the upcoming changes they see in their business and what they feel you need to do to remain as working partners with them.

- **Paid Consultants** - Most large business owners have personal guides, coaches, business consultants. Sometimes they are in a specific field and sometimes they act as general business coaches who can guide you with the complete strategy of your business.

This is one more advantage of meeting people and having your story ready as those who will identify with you and start believing in your cause will be more than ready to help you.

You might not have to get a paid consultant until you have reached a particular scale, where not only is it affordable but the right thing to do.

DO YOU OWN A MIND SPACE?

We had spoken about this earlier when we said that it is the demand of today's time to become a specialist and the days of being a generalist are soon getting over.

With the advent of online marketing sites and online consultation services, businesses will definitely need different skills.

An all-purpose store will only be a department store, but as a business owner, you just might need to own a mind space with not only your clients but also with your industry people along with all your stakeholders.

What is that one thing that your company is known for?
OR
What is the one thing you as an individual are known for?

The more specific your answer is, the more number of people will help you grow and reach your full potential.

The competition is for the consumer's mind space and for costs of economy and scale, which is where most micro, small and medium companies are finding themselves losing market share to either the online space or to the larger conglomerates.

Almost like Haldiram means ....

McDonalds means ....

Now .... (put your name here) or the name of your business .... (if it not a personal brand but your business brand which matters to you) **means** ....

Now how do you verify this?

Once again, ask your clients if they feel so...

LESS IS MORE - COLLABORATION IS THE KEY

If what you are known for is a small space and you feel that it reduces your chance for business, success and to achieve your dream, this is where you will realise that you can actually be successful in growing your business at an even more aggressive rate if you have one specialised and dedicated field.

If you see the medical field, doctors have specialisation and most of the time; they work together as a team.

So, when a patient enters critical care in a hospital with multiple problems, different doctors treat him/her for different reasons. They are each billed separately too. That is why we see that doctors have no problem in recommending each other.

Would you agree?

Now, let me also tell you that what I told you above is not completely true as it is only the specialised doctors who get recommended, but on the other hand, the General Physicians, Dentists and other general medical practitioners are still competing in a cut-throat business world.

They still need to get recommendations from their clients, but it is not the same with others in their field.

We, as the business owners, will have to learn from this and do it very quickly in this ever-changing and adapting world.

If you are specifically doing one particular thing and you are the master at that to the extent that you own the mind space of not only the customers but also the other people in your field, then you are ready to leverage your mastery for growth.

If you are a normal business owner playing in the MSME (Micro Small and Medium Enterprises) space, we have limited resources. So, if we keep expanding our offerings, we cannot afford to keep hiring resources for the same, who could be experts in that field.

In the end, what it results in is one of 3 choices -

1. Keep playing in a smaller field with smaller projects.

2. Take all the clients requests and then do some things really well and the others with the limited resources we have and give limited options.

3. The third choice is that we outsource it to others and get the work done by an outside expert.

The Third choice ends up being the most preferred choice as you keep expanding and you have to outsource part of the work.

This is where, if the same work starts getting done in "Collaboration" you start ensuring that business also flows both ways.

The starting step for this could be to refer the client to these other specialists who do not do what you do or like you are ready to be masters of their field.

CONTACT SPHERE TO ACCELERATION

Understanding the concept of Contact Sphere, So How do you find such collaborators?

There is a concept called "contact sphere" which can help you with this.

This concept is the reason why networking organisations like BNI and others are able to leverage the power of working together and are able to help the members massively if the right teams get built in the group (called chapter).

"A contact sphere is a set of business owners who deal with the same set of clients or the same target market but do not compete with each other"

Out of this contact sphere, you can easily pick some of them who could work with you easily as they also are specialists in their field and you too are the master of yours.

So, together you can provide the service to the same client and help each other grow your business.

You need to think about it as to who could be the business owners that you might need to develop and strengthen relationships with so that your businesses are working out together?

Let's try and find some for your business also…

Target Market no 1

Target market chosen - *(please try and make this as specific as possible)*

....

....

The other business owners who would be looking for clients from this same market

1. ....

2. ....

3. ....

Target Market no 2

Target market chosen - *(please try and make this as specific as possible)*

....

....

....

The other business owners who would be looking for clients from this same market

4. ....

5. ....

6. ....

Target Market no 3

Target market chosen - *(please try and make this as specific as possible)*

....

....

....

The other business owners who would be looking for clients from this same market

7. ....

8. ....

9. ....

Now some of you might have only 1 or 2 target markets, so please feel free to expand the list below to more than 3 business owners from that market.

If you start off with trying to find even one person each from these 9 or 10 business owners whom you can align your business with, it would be the first step of working together as a team.

We started this book with the idea that more people should know about your story and your work.

This would be a good way now that you are not sharing your story only, but there are other people who share your story too.

You can use your SAV statement with them to build relationships and also share the "why" of your business.

If your ideas align, you will find that you will be able to work better.

Furthermore, if you know what you stand for, what you want to do and where you want to go; finding like-minded people who would also want to walk or even run along with you becomes easier.

With this, your story gets spread even faster and your reputation starts getting built even faster than you could do when being all alone.

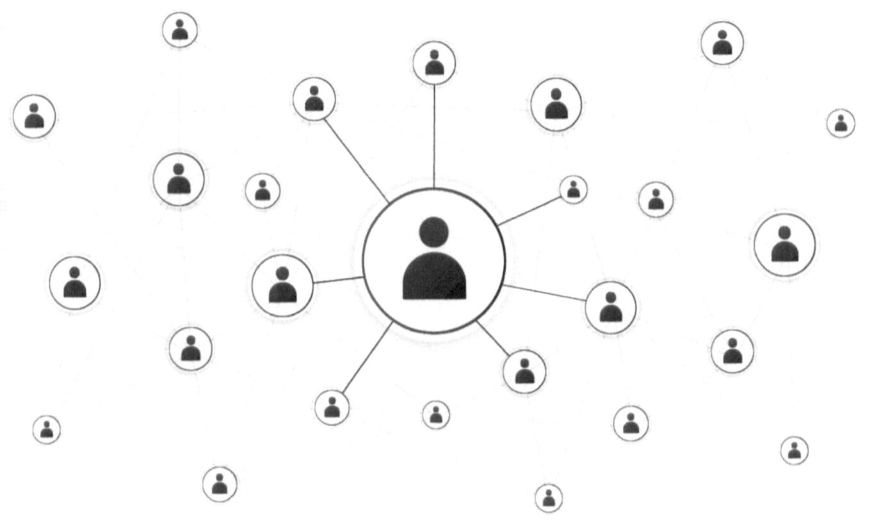

CHAPTER

Eight

Who you Meet will define who you can be

So, if you have reached this far in the book, you must have got an idea of how to speak about your business and look at the future of your goals or vision of life..

In the last section, we explored the prospects of meeting people.

Not every person, but the right person will help you achieve these goals more easily.

This chapter will help you understand this concept in a better manner. It will help you set up a network around you to make you successful.

The online story

The world around us is rapidly changing. There have been many different phases of change and I will try and capture this process in this one single diagram.

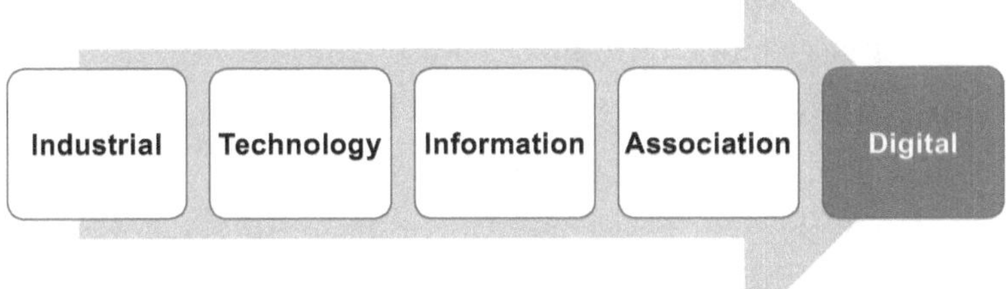

Across the years, companies created valuations due to the changing economy.

Different people define it differently, but the easiest way I could understand this is by checking which companies are getting the most valuations on the stock market at that point of time.

- **Industrial Revolution**

  During this period, the manufacturing companies created the most value and companies like Ford Motors and GM had the most highest valued shares in the market.

  These companies are here to exist as they produce goods which will be required by us forever, though the specifications and the use might change.

- **Technological Revolution**

  In this period, companies like Infosys, IBM and Apple ruled the stock markets and had some of the highest market shares, which are still a part of our lives.

  Some of the companies went redundant also, like Blackberry, Canon and even Nintendo and are now trying to re-invent themselves.

- **Information Revolution**

  In this period, companies like Google were bagging the highest share prices with the maximum returns and even now they are in demand.

  Although they have to keep being agile to remain in the lead and also need to keep acquiring innovative companies and create huge departments existing for new innovations.

- **Association Age**

As Technology and Innovation became a normal part of our lives, we as human beings also evolved. Our generation is a part of this new period(for ease I have named it as the age of associations).

Companies like Facebook overtook Google in their valuations, even in the stock market. This is the theme with new apps, also connecting and the world has started becoming smaller.

- **Digital Age**

I started writing this book before the Covid Lockdown and was only stopping myself at the above 5 different eras, but in this period of social distancing and no travel and lockdowns, we have just sowed the seeds for the Digital Age.

Once again, the markets are rewarding companies which are able to digitally enhance and support their business and this is going to be the new age Reality of tomorrow.

I saw this picture in an article and I hope this will support my view:-

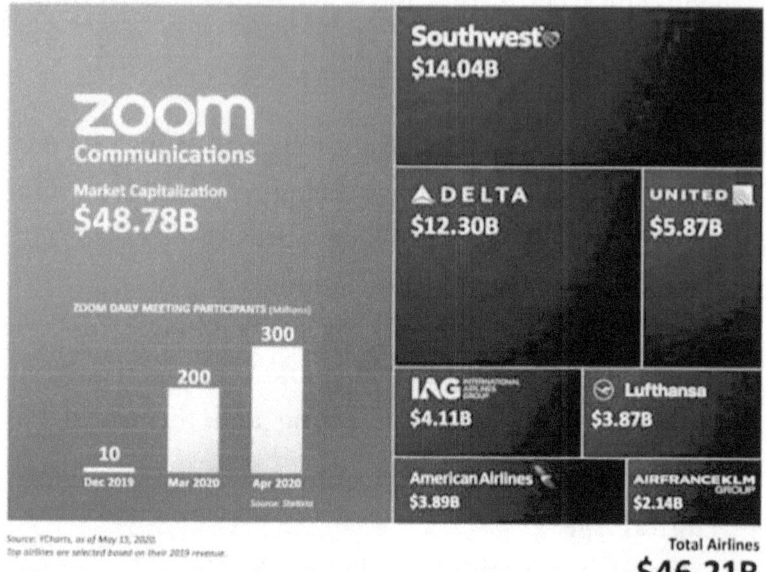

The value of zoom, which was an online meeting platform, has overtaken the value of the top 5 airline companies of the world put together. I know that this might be a temporary phenomenon and things will return back to normal, but huge valuations have got created in this period of time also.

Every new venture builds on the earlier periods and in this digital age, we are relying even more on associations.

That is the reason that I have a feeling that it could be the start of a new era in time.

All the time invested in the work above and in changing some of your communication thoughts is going to be even more useful for the current period.

You will not only have to define clearly "what you do" and "why you do", but you will also have to be a master of your game to start thinking of disrupting the industry or entering an industry which will disrupt the marketplace with a focussed approach.

NETWORKING IS THE FASTER VALUE CREATOR.

The whole purpose of any business is to create value. And if you have seen the valuations story, let me paint another picture for you:

Let's compare some valuations of companies – (Please note that these valuations are from 2019 and could be different today after the Covid 19 viurs has affected us all)

SET 1 - ROAD TRANSPORTATION INDUSTRY OR COMMUTING INDUSTRY- We shall take 2 companies for this purpose over here -	
HONDA MOTORS	**UBER**
2019 valuation of **US$ 42.1 Billion** approx.	2019 valuation of **US$ 66 Billion** approx
They have numerous manufacturing facilities and also various plants around the world and they need to maintain manpower and inventory.	They have almost no inventory and limited manpower on their rolls as employees. They don't own a single car for providing service.

SET 2 - HOTELS INDUSTRY
Let's take 2 companies again over here.

MARRIOTT HOTELS	AIR BnB
2019 Valuation of **US$ 17.08 Billion** approx.	2019 Valuation of **US$ 30 Billion** Approx.
They have to pay rent, have staff and need to maintain and upkeep their properties around the world.	They do not own a single property as a hotel to rent out and do not have the staff to maintain the properties.

SET 3 - SHOPPING (MULTI ITEM SORES)
Time to compare 2 companies again

WALMART	AMAZON
2019 Valuation of **US$ 260 Billion** Approx.	2019 Valuation of **US$ 702 Billion** Approx.
One of the largest departmental store chains around the world with multiple outlets and multi-formatted stores. Have to pay rent and of course again hire loads of people to service their stores	Most of us would have tried shopping online from this store. Now they maintain inventory and have started their own brand products, but essentially they are a very small part of the complete sales volume of the store. Their rent and staff are limited to the logistics need only.

From all the above examples, we learn that the world is changing around us and the valuations are being created differently now.

We have a new word in our dictionary which we must have never heard about before a few years called "*Aggregators*".

What are aggregators?

"A person or organization that collects information from the internet pages of other businesses and puts it on a single website" - Cambridge Dictionary

I would like to explain it as a personal or organisational website that brings a network of sellers and buyers together.

It is a collaboration between product manufacturers or traders with the technology or digital platform providers with logistics firms to link the seller to a buyer.

This collaboration, as you can see, is creating unbelievable valuations as it links the benefits provided with the people needing the benefits.

A successful aggregator is the one who is able to let the people buy and choose their benefits in a better manner or technologically make the search easier for the users.

The 3 main words I can see over here are:

Collaborators

Networks

Benefits

THE VALUE OF HAVING THE RIGHT PEOPLE AROUND YOU

I hope you were able to relate the above section with what we have covered in the book so far and this chapter is like the cherry on the ice cream.

It inspires you to bring it all together so that you can not only tell your story but make sure that it is heard on a wider platform and you also get the benefit of achieving your SAV through that.

Today, the power of networking and compounding your relations is even more important so that you can achieve your goals and you begin to realise your vision of your life.

All of us already have these networks around us right now.

If you have not been exposed to structured networking, you might not have thought about this before.

The easiest way to understand this through this mind-map which makes you think about all the contacts that you might be having and putting them on one big sheet.

This mind-map is given in appendix no 2.

This sheet becomes even more fun if you take a print out in A3 size paper and start filling it in.

If you think about it, every place where you meet people on a regular basis is a place where you can network.

It can start with your family and then it may lead to how you keep growing your networks. Just in case, if you did not do the exercise in appendix 2, let me take you to an easy way to think about this.

The first network you were born with is your family and so let's start with that:

1. Your **family members**

2. Your **extended family members**

   Then you went outside in the real world and met more people and as you kept meeting them and playing with them as a child, so your network grew and now you had another network called.

3. Your **Friends** - neighbourhood, school, college, post-graduation friends etc.

   If You started working, you got another network over there.

4. Your **Work Colleagues**

   The chances are that if you are reading this book, you must be in business and so another set of networks opened up to you.

5. Your **Associates**

6. Your **Clients**

7. Your **Suppliers**

8. Your **Staff** also

   Then you started socializing as an adult and wanted to connect with like-minded people who were interested in the same activities as you were. These could be so many starting from the gym you regularly go to your hobbies like biking or sketching and even clubs and other places of interest.

9. Your **Common Interest Groups** - Biking, Sketching, Gym, etc

10. Your **Professional Groups** - ICAI, Engineers associations, Chambers of commerce, MCCIA, etc.

11. Your **Social Networking groups** - Rotary, Lions, etc.

12. Your **Community Groups** - JITO, MPI, religious groups.

Some of you must have also wanted to become a part of the structured referral and business support groups.

13. Structured Networking Groups - EO, YPO, BNI, etc.

Now there are 2 ways to look at this and even if you take a count of the people you have listed, they could easily be between 500 to 1000.

So, of course, it starts with networking with the right people, but there is more to this.,

POWER OF COMPOUNDING OF RELATIONSHIPS

Networking is not only connecting with these people, but it is also you having *"access to their connections".*

Like you, the people you know also have the same kind of connections like you do and if you calculate, the power of 1 good contact is equivalent to getting a connection into their network of a 1000 people that they must be knowing.

Networking enables you to build trust with these people, that they would then also be ready to connect you to their network.

MEETING PEOPLE WITH INTENTION & NOT ACCIDENT.

We all have a list of close to 500 to 1000 people that we are able to get in touch with easily, but it might not be possible to maintain connections with all of them.

There have been many social scientists who have studied this in detail and the primary accepted studies were done by an anthropologist called Robin Dunbar in the 1990s.

Robert Dunbar is known for what is famously known as **Dunbar's number**.

Dunbar's number is a suggested cognitive limit to the number of people with whom one can maintain stable social relationships.

The relationships in which an individual knows who each person is and how each person relates to every other person.

Dunbar gave us The Rule Of 150.

The Rule of 150 states that the size of an effective network is limited to 150 members. Social scientists theorize that 150 is the limit of the human ability to remember and respond to all the relationships that he has with the people around him. The human mind seems unable to maintain a large number of distinct relationships.

Now that we've established that, we can only handle a limited number of relationships, it's a good strategy to pick and choose them wisely. This may sound somewhat harsh, but it might be time for a "relationship audit."

Figure out who inspires and motivates you. Conversely, identify those who bore you or stress you out. Find ways to spend more time with the people who are positive influencers and decrease the bandwidth given to those who could have negative effects.

This might also be time to identify those people who can help you take you closer to your vision.

I always crack this joke that if you are married, then 50 out of the 150 are almost given because you have to maintain the relationships with relatives and especially your in-laws. As an Indian with large complex family structures, this is even more applicable.

You might say that you have limited choices with your suppliers and also your clients as they are not in your control.

What about friends you might ask? You have friends from college and school and you have been hanging out with them forever and just because I have come along and I am saying that you have to maintain relationships with only some people, it is not right to end lifelong relationships.

So, let me explain my perspective.

We need people around us for many reasons and I like to simplify it with this diagram.

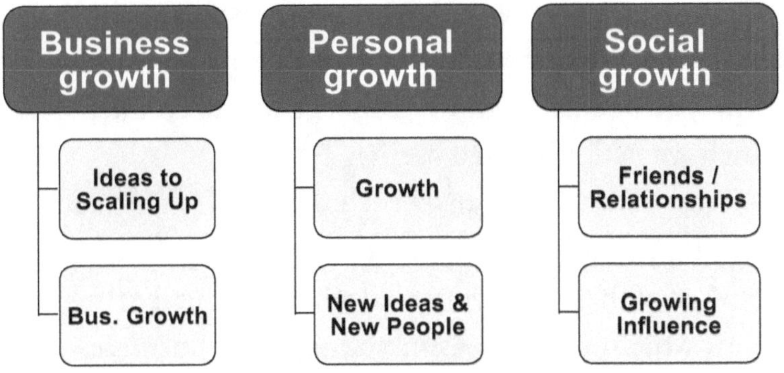

This is a very simplified way of organising your thoughts relating to the needs of people around us and by no means, I am saying that this covers all our needs for people around us as we are more complex than this simplified diagram.

However, just to organise your thoughts, we need people for 3 main reasons around us where our personal well being and growth are considered.

So, let me explain this diagram to you.

The 3 main reasons why we need people in our life for growth and happiness are:

1. For Business Growth Reasons

You need people to help you grow your current business with this set of people. Your customers, your suppliers and your associates will fit in this group and you need to be in regular touch with them so that you could keep running your business.

Now there could be a few people amongst this set itself, or maybe you might need another set of people for helping you get ideas to grow your business. This might also include competitors or also other allied industries or maybe people from the concept of the contact sphere which we had discussed earlier.

This list could also include paid help such as consultants and also unpaid mentors and guides.

Most of them are connected with your current business, its growth and new ideas in your current business.

At times, they can give you ideas for a new business too, but for clarity, I like the idea of putting them into the next list.

2. For Personal Growth Reasons

This set of people are needed for your personal growth and they are people who help you keep developing as a person or as a business owner.

Here growth is defined in 2 ways and that is why it is personal growth and they are for your growth as a person and what new traits or qualities that you need to develop or what new do you need to learn so that you can elevate your performance as a person.

This could be related to work, your hobbies or your interest.

Over here, the other set of people you need is for getting new ideas for work. It could be a completely different line of work compared to your current business, or it could be another business associated with your current line of work.

These are those people who make you think and also

people who light up the fire inside you and give you lots of ideas.

3. For Social Reasons

Finally, the third set of people you need around you are for your personal reasons or social reasons and it is also for your basic human needs of love, connections, relaxation and also for esteem.

Over here also, for ease of recognising these people, I have divided them into 2 sections and that is for friendship or connections and for esteem.

The first set of people you need over here are for maintaining your connection with others and the feeling of belonging.

They could be friends, relatives and also your loved ones really close to you. You need them for either relaxing or for fulfilling your emotional needs.

The other set of people you need over here are to increase your connections and for improving your reputation. They help you by fulfilling your needs to be recognised and can connect you to your recognition.

They increase your centre of influence as you are known as an expert in your field.

Now are these set water-tight compartments?

Not necessarily and there could be some people who could be fulfilling more than one need in more than even one of the basic needs and that is completely okay.

By now, I hope you are aware that there are people you need for different reasons in life.

You also must have got convinced that there are only a finite number of relationships that you can maintain easily at every point of time with investing reasonable amounts of time in doing so.

I hope you must have also got a little bit of an idea that maintaining these relationships is something you will do with intention and not by accident which means that you will be investing your time to maintain, nurture and grow these relationships.

This will help you reach closer to your goal and vision of your life.

Some of you must be wondering by now, that I meet lots of new people and that I have all my needs covered and so why do I need to do this thing called a relationship audit?

My question to you is that are you socialising or are you networking? We shall discuss this more in the last chapter of our journey together through this book.

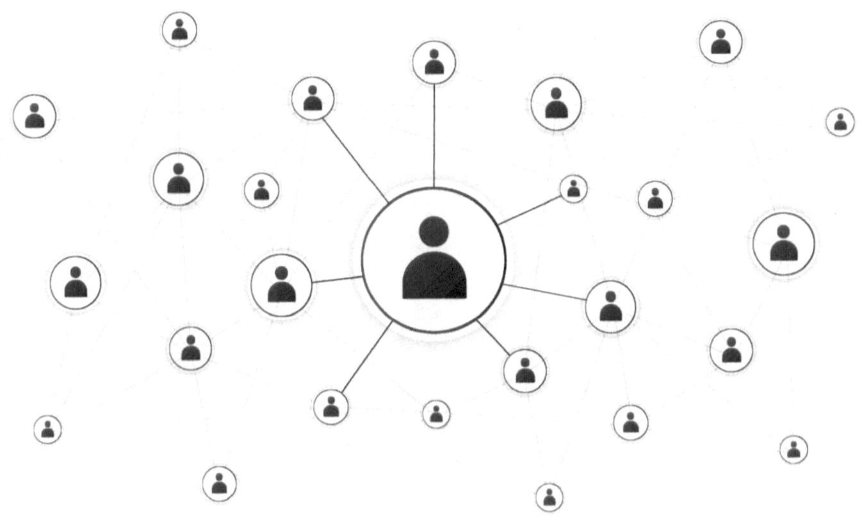

CHAPTER
Nine

Making Your Relationships Count

DIFFERENCE BETWEEN SOCIALISING AND NETWORKING?

Socialising is meeting a lot of people and we do not pay special attention to it. In fact, we do it randomly at various parties, events and occasions.

Then you must be wondering as to what is networking?

Networking is meeting people with a "Goal" and "Purpose". It is not random but thought off and the logical purpose is that it helps us achieve our goals or vision.

Networking is not accidental but intentional.

The easiest way I explain this is by an example of a wedding invitation of a relative that you must have received. If it is an Indian wedding, you can easily expect around 500 guests at the reception.

Now you are not sure who is coming and who has been invited as it is out of your control, but you will know lots of people, as it's from a relative network. When you meet them now, it is socialising.

In another scenario, let's say you meet 100 people whom you know and are introduced too. If you have started becoming a networker, you would possibly have at the back of your mind, the thought about meeting the right people and if you realize that even out of the 100 you met and were introduced, there could be 3 people who could be an addition to your network.

You spend your evening devoting more time with them and trying to start off the relationships that you can get a chance to meet again later and get the relationship going.

Here, you change the socialising scenario into a networking scenario.

I hope that you would also agree with this statement - *"It is not only the width of your network that matters but more importantly it is the depth of the network"* for achieving your goals and vision.

RELATIONSHIP AUDITS

Albert Einstein says *"Insanity is doing the same thing over and over and expecting different results."*

So if you want different results, you will need to start working with your relationships also differently.

I had briefly mentioned this in the earlier chapter but would like to spend some more time on this as this is where all this starts coming together to help you.

SHORT RELATIONSHIPS AUDIT -

I hope my point is clear that you would invest the time to re-think your network and spend 15 mins on this exercise that I recommend for you as an easy start to this journey.

Here we have identified 6 basic needs for which you need people and let's try and find the first set of people that you are going to work with.

Are you ready to begin identifying people for your growth now?

(A) FOR BUSINESS GROWTH

How many people can you identify in each category?

(a) Clients who are existing but could buy more often if you had better relationships with them. How many can you identify?

(b) Prospects who are not your clients but might become if you get introduced to them. Who can introduce you to them?

(c) Suppliers who could introduce you to good clients and you would want to build relationships with them.

(d) Suppliers whom you need to build relationships with, as they are critical for your operations and you want to build your relationship with them.

(e) Associates who could help grow your business and you need to maintain relationships with them.

(f) Which people can help you get ideas to grow your business and can be your mentors and you need to build your relationships with them?

(g) Who are the people who can introduce you to people who can give you ideas to grow in your business or industry?

(h) Whom can you hire to help you grow your business in areas where you might be stuck?

(i) Can you identify more people in different categories who can help you grow your business right now or by giving some ideas? Add them here.

(B) FOR PERSONAL GROWTH

How many people can you identify who can help you grow personally?

(a) Do you know an expert in your business around you?

(b) Do you know an expert in your industry around you?

(c) Do you know anyone who has knowledge about the economy and can give you ideas of what is happening in the economy?

(d) Who are those people who meet a lot of people and can update you about the upcoming trends or ideas?

(e) Who do you have in your circle who likes to read a lot of information about the future of business or disruption?

(f) Making it broader, who do you know who reads a lot in the areas which you want to grow in and is ready to give you some time to listen to you and speak to you?

(g) Do you have an accountability partner if you have a new project that you are thinking off?

(h) Who are people from your network who inspire and motivate you and you like to listen to them?

(i) Who do you think has a personality that you would like to have? They might be good at convincing, or in public speaking or they have a calm personality. You like the way they speak, or they are all fired up and you want to be like them. They should definitely be in the network that you want to maintain.

(j) Do you want to do something besides your business but which is work-oriented and what is that?

If it is writing a book, you have to hang out with the people who write books so that you get inspired to finish our book (This one worked for me as 2 people just kept pushing me till I finished the book. Thank you Kailash Pinjani and Anand Mahurkar)

Let's think about things other than a business where you want to grow and include an activity or a hobby now.

(k) What do you want to become better at?

Who are the people you know that are good at that? You will need to spend time with them or have them as a part of your network.

(l) If you want to start exercising, you will need friends who make you commit to exercise and hold you accountable.

A fabulous example of this is KVT Ramesh, founder of *Pick a Book* and also a serial entrepreneur who inspired the whole of the BNI leadership not only across India but across many countries committed to exercise.

Thanks to him, I have a fixed limit of doing 7000 steps every day and actually got a band around my wrist, which makes sure that it reminds me.

(m) Do you want to start doing something new like painting?

You will need people around you and spend time with for that. My wife taught me this, as she wakes me up on Sunday early morning, which I hate, but I go with her to the Sketching Club.

She is a part of the club called the "Urban sketchers" and this inspires her to sketch and even paint. She is really good at that, but she had given it up as she was busy doing other things.

(n) Pick other growth places and the people in your life who do that and keep them close to you. Try to have a network with them and this will help you too.

(C) SOCIAL CIRCLE -

These will be the set of people who will be a part of your social circle and you want to network with them for reasons other than given above.

How many people do you know like that?

(a) Your Relatives

(b) Your Friend Circle

Though more often than not, I have found that normally once you start making a list like this and taking an audit of your relationships, your friend circle will slowly start changing into the above 4 categories.

Although, there will be times when you will just be okay with people whom you like to let your hair down with.

They could be people with whom you would go for a movie with or to a stand-up comedy show and will not mean that you want to become either of those.

(c) People whom you like to help -

There could be some of you who like to spend time with children or with aged people and volunteer your time for this. It might figure in any of the above, but you would still want these people in your circle as they fit into your other needs.

(d) Religious circles might also fit over here.

For the next set of people, I feel that they are the most important if you want to actually make your reputation.

This set of people might be in one of the other categories, but it is important to keep a separate stock of such people as they might matter the most at different times in your life.

(e) People in your network who are connected with officials that you might need

(f) People in your network who are connected with and can introduce you to people whom you consider as your idols.

(g) People in your network who can get you speaking engagements if you want to be known as an expert in any field.

(h) If you have business ideas, and you need the right people to be able to actually build on it, they could fit in the first set and also over here if you are talking of doing something really different or need to actually meet people of influence.

(i) People who can get you introduced to a circle of people that you might also want to be a part of.

DETAILED RELATIONSHIP AUDIT -

However, if you want to do a detailed audit of your relationships and set yourself up for success in an even stronger manner, I would recommend this detailed exercise that can help you reach your goals and your vision even faster.

STEP 1 -

Fill in the details in appendix 3 in the worksheet of your contacts sheet.

a. Start with identifying your main networks. I have done the exercise of putting the 3 common one over there, which are family, friends and work. Which are the other networks that you belong to from the list given above? It could be from your Gym, or an organisation you belong to.

b. Now fill in the rest of the details with names of people from that network and they should be specific people that you could remember or think of.

STEP 2 -

Let's start doing the relationship audit now of these people, where in front of each person you have to put 1 out of 6 needs by numbering them. In case you feel that the name you have written fits in none of these categories, then leave it blank.

Congratulations that you have completed the basics of knowing who you know and where do they fit in to achieve your goals in your life.

What comes next?

STEP 1 - Are you above the Dunbar number or below it? If you are above 150, then you might have to start thinking of whom you would like to strengthen your relationship based on what is your current requirement of what need is important for you to fulfil.

STEP 2 - If you are below the Dunbar number, congratulations to you as you have lots of room in your life to meet new people and build your relationships in a manner that could be of great help for you to reach your goals.

STEP 3 - Make a list of people you have a relationship fit into with only 1 or maybe even 2 of your needs?
Is that consistent with your vision and your goals that you have identified?

STEP 4 - You will now consciously know who are those set of people that you will need to start introducing into your network. Knowing is the first step.

STEP 5 - Who are those people right now in your network who can get your first introduction to these people, so that you could start building this network also which you have now realised is missing. This may be keeping you away from those stepping stones, which lead to your success.

STEP 6 - Even if you find no one, where will you now need to hang out to start relationships without introduction. This is not a part of networking, but sometimes one needs to start new networks and that has to be done consciously from scratch.

Which organisations will you have to join for such introductions or which places will such people visit more often to self introduce yourself?

A word of caution over here, that if you do this exercise

once, it is not for a lifetime as our needs keep changing with time and so does your relationships and the people in your circle.

It might be perfectly okay to change the list with time.

The Internet Is Dunbar's Multiplier.

While it's extremely difficult to maintain hundreds of personal relationships, the internet has made the task a little bit easier.

Sure, emails are not the same as handshakes — but they give us the ability to keep track of our relationships more efficiently. The worldwide web also enables us to easily find people with the knowledge we need.

Finally, social media is a catalyst for multiplying your personal Dunbar's number. With LinkedIn, you can keep track of contacts, on Quora, you can crowdsource a question and with Twitter, you can follow smart people sharing smart ideas.

THE EASIEST WAY OF GAINING TRUST

We have covered so much ground by now that I will now only be getting in your way if I make you read too much more on this as you have followed the process to -

* Setting your goals and vision - to know where we want to go.
* After that, we took a journey down the road of learning to speak about ourselves. And even about our goals and vision.
* We did a brief of what to talk to and to whom.

* Then we went on a journey of finding the one who will help you achieve these goals and vision.
* We have now got your action plan of who would you actively work with and keep a connection within your network.
* Finally, we ended up also getting to know where we need to start a network.

Where do we go from here?

If you ask me, I would advise you to start working on building your relationships and communicating with them in a manner that can achieve your goals and vision in life.

However, to do that, you will need very small basics of how to build trust with this set of people and how do you not only start an introductory relationship at times or have a relationship for maybe a lifetime.

It's time to make it stronger now, but I will leave you with some thoughts on what you need to do now through some suggestions given below to give you a basic guide to start discovering your way.

What do you do to build Trust?

I. The first and the easiest thing you can do is stay in touch with them.

II. Call them, speak to them and maybe even meet them at regular intervals and not only when you have work.

Differentiate between work conversations and relationship-building conversations.

III. The most important part is to find out about them? Ask them about themselves and then listen and take notes.

IV. If need be, dedicate a journal for your network of 150 pages - 1 page per person.
Note down the following details about them -
a. Their family details
b. Their birthday and anniversary
c. Their postal address (home or office, anyone will do based on your relationships with them)
d. Their business
e. What are they interested in and what are their hobbies
f. Their goals
g. Their vision
h. What kind of introductions will help them?
i. How could you help them with something that matters to them not only for right now but for where they might want to go in their life in future.

V. Don't trust your memory but keep updating this journal. Realise that 150 people are a lot in number and it is a lot of information to keep in your head.

VI. You are not going to get all the details at one go and so maybe you need to keep maintaining it for a really long period of time to get people to open up to you as you show interest in them. Some information might change with time too.

VII. Show Interest in them and let them know that you would like to know more about them, what they care about and do not be surprised if it has changed from the last time you met them or you heard or understood something different from what they meant.

That was the easy part.

Who amongst us does not like having good soulful meaningful conversations with others as it feels human and alive after we have such a conversation with another human being?

What will help you build this trust with them easily once you have collected this information?

Here are a few suggestions-

1. Wish them on their occasions. There are auto email programs which help you do this. Or if you befriend them on Facebook, it will make sure that you do not forget.

   Don't just say happy Birthday but make it personal by adding a line about them being able to achieve their wish or improve their health or what they had said is their goal.

2. Send them Information which interests them - If you are reading something that might be of interest to what they need or want to know, send them information to them when you come across such information or such an article.

   Digital life has made it so much easier to do this with social apps.

3. Give them a Thank you Card - If they do something for you which is special, send them a hand-written thank you card. If the favour is really big, try giving the card personally or send it by courier, Yes you read that right. Email is new normal and so you act abnormally.

4. Surprise them - Send something to them for no reason except to say hello. This does not have to be big but something they might like

5. All of the above is useful but if you want to build a strong relationship with someone, one of the most important things to do is MAKE INTRODUCTIONS.

Since this is so important, I would like to cover this in a separate section altogether though it is going to be a really small one.

MAKING INTRODUCTIONS

In BNI, our philosophy is "Givers Gain®".

It is also called - "what goes around comes around" or "law of reciprocity".

The law of reciprocity basically says that when someone does something nice for you, you will have a deep-rooted psychological urge to do something nice in return.

As a matter of fact, you may even reciprocate with a gesture far more generous than their original good deed.

So, if you want the people in your network to introduce you to the right people, to help you reach closer to your goals and fulfil your vision, work at helping them achieve their goals too.

The fastest way to build trust is to find out where they would like to get introduced and then start working your network and their networks together. By this, you could try and get an introduction possible for this person you want to strengthen and deepen the relationship with so that they also would want to do the same for you.

You will have to do the work first.

Give to the relationship first. Feed it.

TIME INVESTED VERSUS TIME SPENT IS THE SECRET TO YOUR FUTURE SUCCESS

Now some of you might be thinking that it was okay for me to do all the hard work and to learn how to speak to the right people in the right way and also than identifying and finding the right people.

But now he says (that is me by the way!) that I will have to spend even more time on this.

As it is, we all have enough things to do in life and then adding one more to the list, that seems unfair and not doable.

I completely agree with you, my friend!

So, here is the deal.

How about spending just 15 mins of 1 day every 6 months dedicated to one of the strong networks that you need to help you achieve your vision.

Also for following up on the connection that could help by making only 2 or 3 phone calls or sending 1 or 2 emails for them?

Let's do the maths -

This is for 1 person for 1 year.

S. NO OF ACTIVITY	ACTIVITY	TIME INVESTED
1.	Meeting 2 times a year	120 mins
2.	Call every month	10 mins times 10 = 100 mins
3.	Follow up for them	15 mins times 3 times = 45 mins
4.	Incidental activities like birthdays, anniversary, thank you notes	30 mins
	TOTAL TIME	**295 Min per person per year = 300 mins if we round it off**

Now that seems like a hell of a lot and if you multiply this with even 100 people rounding it off to 300 mins, it is 30000 mins a year.

I can almost hear you think, 30,000 mins. Seriously, that is a lot of time!!!

So, let me put this in perspective -

30,000 mins out of 525600 mins in a year.

That is 5.7% of your total time. Let's round it off to 6% of your total time.

Now, it is totally up to you to adjust the times that are needed for different people and you can decide that and also adjust it accordingly to the needs that you have for today and what is important to you right now.

Just one word of caution though; that if you only build relationships with people for your today, how will your tomorrow even start?

You have 2 choices in life.

Either you can spend this 6% of your time to network and grow relationships so that you can intentionally grow your relationships with people who will help you achieve your goals and your vision of your life.

OR

You could choose to keep toiling away like that lone wolf who has to keep working hard doing what he wants to do.

I hope that this will also make you realise that on whom you need to spend your time, will either make you or break you.

Will it open the door to your future, or do you want to keep banging on doors all alone meeting more dead ends?

The choice is yours to make.

And if you have made the right choice, it might be time to go to the very start of this book and take out that pencil and get a notebook ready.

Let's build our lives as per our choice as the choice is

truly in your hands.

Thank you for coming along with me on this journey of building your life through your life-story!

Remember, to connect with others and to reach your goals and the vision of your life, as;

"It Starts With You"

Appendix 1

To download, please visit www.BharatDaga.com

Appendix 2

168 Planner Template							
	Mon	Tues	Wed	Thurs	Fri	Sat	Sun
4:00 / 4:30							
4:30 / 5:00							
5:00 / 5:30							
5:30 / 6:00							
6:00 / 6:30							
6:30 / 7:00							
7:00 / 7:30							
7:30 / 8:00							
8:00 / 8:30							
8:30 / 9:00							
9:00 / 9:30							
9:30 / 10:00							
10:00 / 10:30							
10:30 / 11:00							
11:00 / 11:30							
11:30 / 12:00							
12:00 / 12:30							
12:30 / 13:00							
13:00 / 13:30							
13:30 / 14:00							
14:00 / 14:30							
14:30 / 15:00							
15:00 / 15:30							
15:30 / 16:00							
16:00 / 16:30							
16:30 / 17:00							
17:00 / 17:30							
17:30 / 18:00							
18:00 / 18:30							
18:30 / 19:00							
19:00 / 19:30							
19:30 / 20:00							
20:00 / 20:30							
20:30 / 21:00							
21:00 / 21:30							
21:30 / 22:00							
22:00 / 22:30							
22:30 / 23:00							
23:00 / 23:30							
23:30 / 0:00							
0:00 / 0:30							
0:30 / 1:00							
1:00 / 1:30							
1:30 / 2:00							

To download, please visit www.BharatDaga.com

Appendix 3

Name:
Business:
Specialization:
FAMILY
FRIENDS
B2B
FATHER
MOTHER
SPOUSE
SCHOOL
COLLEGE
OTHERS
VENDORS
ASSOCIATES
CLIENTS

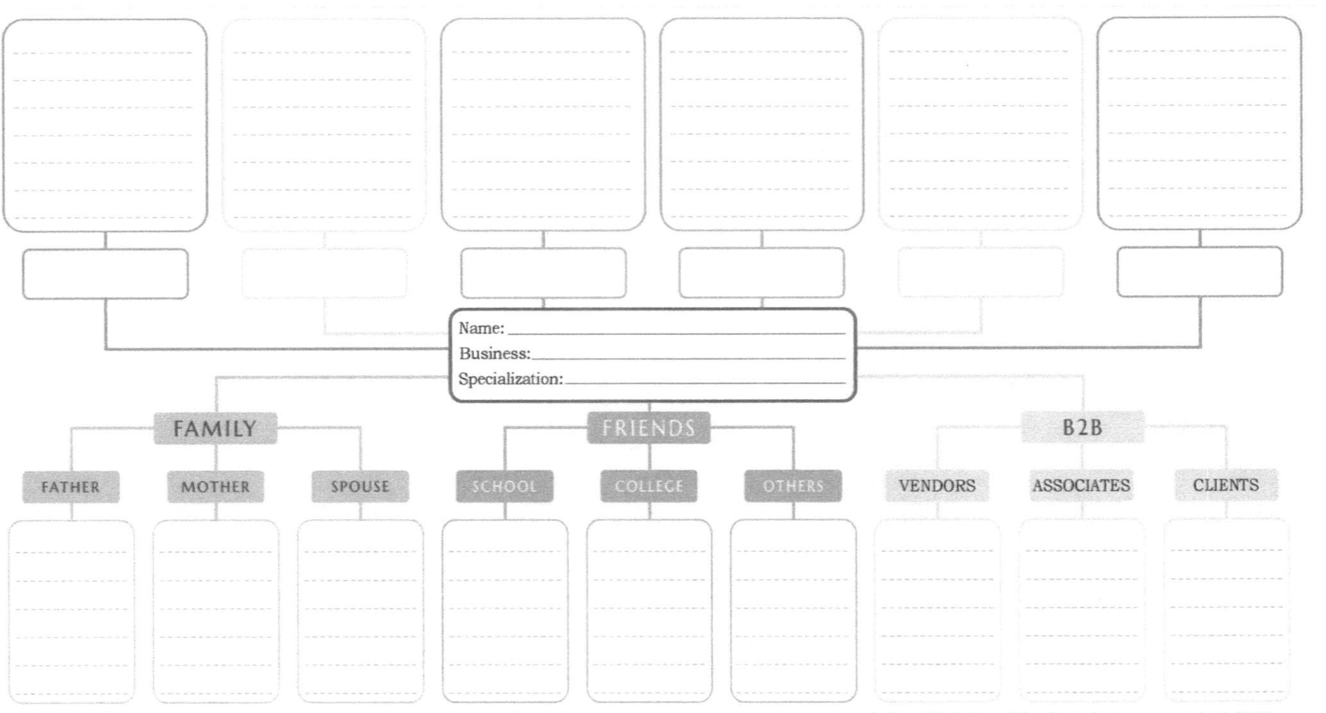

About Author

Bharat is an aspiring author contributing to magazines on articles on networking.

- Bharat is a serial entrepreneur who was involved in the marketing of various products like Textiles, Floppy Diskettes, Wheat Flour, Pharma consumables, financial products, etc.

- He has been a trainer in Organizations like ICICI Prudential Life Insurance, Idea Cellular, Cummins, QED and many others on topics like sales & marketing and motivational growth and is also called as a keynote speaker at events and in educational institutions.

- Currently, he is also the Co-Executive Director of BNI in Pune region which is one of the top regions in the world and he works with close to 1500 entrepreneurs as members who have generated 736 crores of business through structured networking in the year 2019 alone.

- Bharat is also the National Trainer for BNI India and has been invited to train and coach about networking at national and international events in other countries.

- Bharat is also serving on Apex decision making bodies across BNI Internationally, which formulates a strategy for how to make networking more impactful in BNI.

- The exposures of Bharat to these higher roles have helped study best practices of how to develop organisational culture and team management through breakthrough thinking processes.

- He was also awarded the CEO Award in 2018 for his contribution to the development of best practices to support business owners in BNI worldwide.

PERSONAL INFORMATION:

- He is a voracious reader who believes in Continuous education and Up-gradation of Knowledge.
- Activities of interest: Traveling around the world and seeing new places, meeting new people and experiencing new cultures and he loves trying out new foods as he is a self-confessed "foodie."
- Bharat believes that new experiences one of the best forms of learning and is what keeps him alive. He has done sky-diving, Jumped off a building, gone scuba diving, river rafting and tried out various weird food across the world and the next thing he wants to get off his bucket list is to go bungee jumping off a bridge on top of a river.
- His professional desire is to create a community of business owners who are the team for business owners to be able to succeed together and live a happy and successful life with less stress and more time with the people they care about and love.

About Book

An entrepreneurs journey is normally a very lonely journey, but it does not have to be so. This book starts with you and discovering your passion in business and then connects what you are to connecting with people around you in a powerful manner so that you can have a team of people around you who are your connects and contacts.

This is a book is about how to succeed by knowing you and your message and connecting it with your contacts around you so that you can live the life of your dreams and achieve your desires, dreams and goals for your life. This book is a mix between practical examples, stories and also exercises so that you can practically take a step by step journey of discovering you, your passion and then learn how to use that connect to people.

The aim is for you to have a plan ready of how to achieve your dreams by the time you complete this book. This book is a distillation of ideas, learnings, training and readings across the last 30 years of an entrepreneur through a journey of practical experiences of finding how to make entrepreneurship an easier and happier journey.

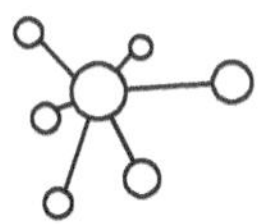

www.ingramcontent.com/pod-product-compliance
Lightning Source LLC
Chambersburg PA
CBHW051435130726
47987CB00005B/2053